The Change

Insights into Self-Empowerment

Jim Lutes ~ Jim Britt

With

Co-authors

Co-authors

Dr. Jon Haass

Staci Boyer

Mariah Sievers

Sally Holmes Reed

Dr. Tianna Conte & Rev. Azima Jackson

Janice Angela Burt

Steve Hultquist

Karen Marshall

Jim Dudas

Mary Lynn Ziemer

Carmen Taylor

Kasey Higbee

Lucas Robak

Peggy Caruso

Max Higbee

Terry Morgeson

Debbie Anderson

Flora Sofia

The Change

Jim Britt ~ Jim Lutes

All Rights Reserved

Copyright 2014

The Change

10556 Combie Road, Suite 6205

Auburn, CA. 95602

The use of any part of this publication reproduced, stored in any retrieval system, or transmitted in any forms or by any means, electronic or otherwise, without the prior written consent of the publisher is an infringement of copyright law.

Jim Lutes ~ Jim Britt

The Change

ISBN   0-9662171-6-0 (paperback)

ISBN   09662171-7-9 (Amazon Kindle)

DEDICATION

This book is dedicated to all those seeking change

Foreword

By Berny Dohrmann, Chairman of CEO Space International

To The Readers of *The Change*

Jim Britt has been a mentor to *Chicken Soup* authors, and to some of the leading thought leaders on earth. Jim Britt's ground breaking work in *Letting Go*, releasing past trauma's and betrayals in life to return once again to forward looking manifestation within your full powers, has been instructed at leading *Fortune* companies and to standing room only seminars all over the world. For three decades, Jim Britt has been the "trainer of the trainers," of which I am only one. Jim has been an instructor at CEO Space, the most prestigious, hard to get into faculty on the planet, where he developed millions of dollars of resources as he assisted others to develop tens of millions of dollars for their own dream making. Jim is the most "unchanged by success and wealth" man I have ever known. He is an unselfish archangel, like in his book *Rings of Truth*.

Today, Jim Britt and Jim Lutes, along with 18 inspiring co-authors from around the world, bring a pioneering work to the market to transform your own journey into master manifestation. Their principles are forged on coaching millions on every continent. As you read, you are exploring self-development as the world has yet to practice. In fact, Jim and Jim's publications lead to this one APEX MOMENT. Everything you have done to date in your own life, everyone you have met, every lesson you have learned, has led you to this one GREAT life opportunity… the moment of your own transformation into ever rising full potentials.

As a five time best selling author myself, as a film maker, and with CEO Space, you can imagine how fussy I am to write a forward to publications in the self-development space. CEO Space was just ranked by Forbes Magazine as the leading entrepreneur firm who hosts five annual business growth conferences, serves over 140 countries, and was ranked as THE MEETING in the world that YOU CAN NOT AFFORD TO MISS by *Forbes*. The world today demands more than a reputation defender to secure your forward brand, it requires that you take responsibility for your own brand and reputation in life. This book will inspire you to do just that.

CEO Space International has supported launches for many amazing works including *Chicken Soup for the Soul, Men Are From Mars, Women Are From Venus, Rich Dad, Poor Dad, The Secret, No Matter What, Three Feet From Gold, Conversations With The King*, and now the movies *Growing Up Graceland* and *Wish Man* (for Make a Wish Foundation), *Outwitting the Devil* by Napoleon Hill and Sharon Lechter, Tony Robbins' great publications, of course Jim Britt's best-selling book *Rings of Truth*; and so many more. The totals have reached more than 2 billion eye balls! You can't play around with that Mount Everest of credibility that I guard like a bank vault!

You can therefore appreciate why I encourage 100% of our followers of all the publications named, to BUY JIM BRITT and JIM LUTES book *The Change* as a customer recognition for your own ten best close relationships or clients. But don't just buy this book, rather I endorse that you buy 10, and you gift wrap them to acknowledge your most important top ten relationships in life, or clients in business. By doing so you will retain more clients and encourage repeat buying. You may also receive more referrals and strengthen each relationship. The laws of giving will come back to you 10 to 1. When you give freely, you will always receive a rain into your life just as you rain into the lives of those you treasure. Jim Britt, Jim Lutes, and the 18 insightful and inspiring co-authors have given you in *The Change*, a great opportunity… more important than pouring ice water over someone's head on YouTube as a challenge for charity! The gift that keeps on giving begins when you step up and BUY 10, knowing you have been instrumental in inspiring 10 friends to live a better life. Together we are going to reach 1 BILLION SOULS as we help Jim Britt, Jim Lutes, and their co-authors to achieve their goal to transform human consciousness in our lifetime. Like Zig Ziglar, Jim Rohn, the great Roger Anthony, and so many friends who have passed, my friend Jim Britt is now an historical event in every training, every publication, and every online work at CEO Space. If you ever have the opportunity, STOP YOUR LIFE and see JIM BRITT & JIM LUTES LIVE and you will thank me personally, I know.

Their work is powerful. You'll let go of the baggage you been carrying around for years and learn to embrace everything that creates the future you want and deserve. As you close the pages of *The Change,* you will say over and over again "THANK YOU Jim Britt and Jim Lutes for creating this work." You will gain a new life of super focus as never before and you will commence to master manifest in your own individual life as never before. *The Change* provides tools to transform results for corporations, institutions and individuals, and once applied it will be impossible to miss your future success in life.

In my opinion, there are only the following areas to embrace for each of us:

- Spiritual oneness and balance

- Recreational balance and nature

- Relationship where *Perfection Can Be Had!* (my book)

- Career attainment of goals you, yourself reset along the way

- Parenting either directly or by embracing a child you adopt to mentor at any and every age in life

These perspectives come into alignment within a framework of Jim Britt and Jim Lutes imagination along with decades of human-potential work. My advice is this work is a "BUY 10 TO SHARE WITH FRIENDS" pledge. In fact, a billion readers is a global path that Jim Britt and Jim Lutes are going to achieve NEXT for the world common good.

Let's help in this quest, as both men unselfishly donate their only asset, their precious LIFE TIME, to elevate one life at a time to their full potential and greatness.

My final request to all those who are reading my forward is that you DO IT NOW. When you think of the good you will be doing, just ask yourself, "How long will I make them WAIT?"

I'm buying my 10 today!

Berny Dohrmann

Chairman, CEO Space International

P.S. I so approve this message for all my readers and followers worldwide. CEO Space has helped authors break the book of all records a half a dozen times, which means the only record to beat can be done with the publication you are buying 10 of now. Together we are going to set a global record with one publication. Make the PLEDGE and give the gift of personal development. DO IT TODAY!

Table of Contents

JIM BRITT	1
THE POWER OF LETTING GO	2
JIM LUTES	11
CREATING YOUR LIFE MASTERPIECE	12
KASEY HIGBEE	21
NAY-SAYERS BE DAMNED!	22
MAX HIGBEE	29
THERE IS NO SUCH THING AS SMALL CHANGE	30
TERRY MORGESON	39
YOUR HEALTH IS A GIFT. DISEASE IS SOMETHING YOU EARN.	40
DR. JON C. HAASS	50
THE CHANGE IN LEADERSHIP	51
CARMEN TAYLOR	61
LIVING BLISSFULLY WEALTHY	62
DEBORAH ANDERSON	73
MY JOURNEY TO COMPASSION	74
JANICE ANGELA BURT	83
JEALOUSY SITS IN MY BONES	84

MARY LYNN ZIEMER 95
EVOLVING YOU: Embrace Happiness to Create the Life of Your Dreams 97
    KAREN MARSHALL 107
THE GOLDEN ERA 108
    STACI BOYER 119
MOTIV8N'U: To Be Your Own Game Changer 120
    LUCAS ROBAK 132
ONLY GOOD CAN COME FROM THIS 133
    STEPHEN HULTQUIST 142
IT'S ALL ABOUT PEOPLE: Business in the Age of Relationships 143
    SALLY HOLMES REED 153
CHANNEL YOUR SUCCESS 154
    PEGGY CARUSO 163
REVOLUTIONIZE YOUR FAMILY'S LIFE 164
    JIM DUDAS 173
GAME CHANGER 174
    DR. TIANNA CONTE & REV M. AZIMA JACKSON, MS, DMin .. 183
EXTRAORDINARY JOURNEY: Conversations Between Two Worlds 185
    FLORA SOFIA 197
THE BEAUTIFUL POWER 198
    MARIAH SIEVERS 207
THE EDGE OF CHANGE: The Three Elements of Conscious Partnership 208
AFTERWORD 217

JIM BRITT

Jim Britt is an internationally recognized leader in the field of peak performance and personal empowerment training. He is author of 13 best-selling books including, *Cracking the Rich Code*, *Cracking the Life Code*, *Rings of Truth*, *The Power of Letting Go*, *Freedom*, *Unleashing Your Authentic Power*, *Do This. Get Rich - For Entrepreneurs*, *The Flaw in The Law of Attraction*, and *The Law of Realization*, to name a few.

Jim has presented seminars throughout the world sharing his success principles and life enhancing realizations with thousands of audiences, totaling over 1,000,000 people from all walks of life.

Jim has served as a success counselor to over 300 corporations worldwide. He was recently named as one of the world's top 20 success coaches and presented with the best-of-the-best award out of the top 100 contributors of all time to the direct selling industry. He also mentored/coached Anthony Robbins for his first five years in business.

Jim is more than aware of the challenges we all face in making adaptive changes for a sustainable future.

THE POWER OF LETTING GO

By Jim Britt

Imagine walking into a room where groups of people are seated at a table where a delicious looking meal was set before them. Their table was filled with every sort of food you could imagine. It's a mouth-watering display, all perfectly prepared and it's all right in front of their noses and easily within their reach.

You notice however, that none of the people are eating. They haven't even taken a single bite. Their plates are empty and it appears that they have been seated there for a very long time, so long that they appear to be starving to death.

They are starving, not because they cannot see or eat all the food before them, or because eating it is forbidden or harmful. They aren't eating because they don't realize that food is what they need. They don't know that those very sharp pains in their stomachs are caused by hunger. They don't see that all they need to do to stop their suffering is eat the food that's right in front of them.

This is an example of our basic human suffering as well. Most of us sense that there is something wrong, something that is inherently missing in our lives, but we haven't a clue how to overcome the problem. We may see faintly that what we need is somehow very close to us, but we don't connect it to the sharp pain inside. Even with time, as the pain becomes even more severe, we start to believe that feeling pain is just a normal part of living.

Let's say you are feeling the pain of unhappiness. You suffer from it daily, not knowing that everything you need to eliminate your suffering and find happiness is making the right choice and letting go. But the problem is that our emotional conflicts are familiar to us and keep us blinded to solutions. We actually become addicted to feeling the way we do, thinking that it is just normal and can't be changed.

The million dollar question for a lot of people is how do we let go and walk away from what's familiar to us? How do we let go of our pain and conflicts. I believe that most people have a desire to do more with their lives, to be happy and not suffer their emotional pains, but most often their fear of the pain of change prevents them from even trying. We very often fear what we want most. And at the same time, we get what we fear most. Our mental programming keeps us safe and secure so we stay where we are. Just look around you. You see it everywhere. People say they want to change but do they really?

Do a little exercise. Take a look at your last five years. Have you truly made progress? Is your last five years what you wanted? Are you where you thought you would be today five years ago? And if not, why not?

When you begin to see the truth behind the conflict, watch what happens to your life. What will happen is that the people, experiences, and opportunities will begin to flow to you and you'll begin to see conflict as just a mental and emotional mistake. Letting go of conflict is a choice. When faced with a conflict, ask yourself this very important question. "What benefit am I getting from holding on to this conflict? Does it serve my higher good? Are you willing to trade an abundant life for hanging onto something that doesn't serve your higher good? Are you willing to spend your vital energy for something that doesn't take you in the direction you want to go?

Many experts say, "just face your fears, do the thing you fear most and the fear will go away." Well, that's easy to say and even makes sense when you hear it. But how about all the people who are afraid to face their fears, too afraid to take the first step? What do they do? What about that buried feeling attached to the fear, what happens to that?

Let's face it, life is risky. Going into business is risky. Getting married is risky… snow skiing, mountain climbing, driving past the speed limit, raising children… I could go on and on. All these are risky, but we do them anyway don't we?

Let's first gain an understanding of the true definition of fear. "Fear is taking a past experience, projecting it into the future with the anticipation of it happening again, and then re-living it in the moment." Fear is simply trapped energy you hold inside that was created from a past traumatic experience, or series of experiences over time. Fear is a mental mistake. It's friction in your thought process. When you get hurt emotionally you feel the pain inside. Then you hold onto that painful experience hoping that it will protect you from it happening again, but it won't.

Fear is simply energy wanting to be released. And once you gain that understanding it becomes easier to let go of the fear.

Fear or love is a choice you make. Look at it this way. Every action you take is either based in fear or love. If you move toward what you love, you naturally move away from what you fear. While you are moving toward what you love and you feel the fear, face it yes, but do more than that. Observe it. Separate yourself from it and see it for what it is, which is just trapped energy patterns created from past experiences coming to the surface wanting to be released. It's your subconscious programming bringing it up saying, "Hey, do you need this anymore or would you like to delete?" Your fear is NOT you. It's just a passenger you have picked up. It is not hanging onto you, instead you are hanging on to it!

When a fear feeling surfaces, breathe into it, and when you exhale, let it go. Then take a course of action that will bring you more of what you love. Just the fact that you have observed yourself feeling the fear, and you see it for what it really is, you have weakened it's hold on you… or rather your hold on it.

Letting go is a choice, moment to moment. It's a fork in the road. It's a choice to buy into the delusion of our mind chatter, of past pains and programming, or move toward what you would love to have in your life.

Remember. Whatever happened to you in the past is not happening to you now unless you let it. The past is only your story and it's not real today. It's a memory, a trapped energy pattern. It's like an old movie that you just keep watching over and over, until you decide you've watched it enough. What's real is the stress headache, anxiety, and unhappiness you've created for yourself out of something that doesn't exist any longer. That's what's real. Think about it.

In order to make any sort of permanent change, whether you want to lose weight, quit smoking, get healthier, earn more money, have a more fulfilling relationship, or break an emotional addictive cycle and eventually be free of it, requires several things.

The first thing required is a desire. You have to want something bad enough in order to make any permanent change. Desire has to come from inside you. No one else can do that for you. I'm assuming that you have a desire to change otherwise you wouldn't be reading this book.

The next step is that you must make a decision to change. It's not important that you know how to change at this point, but it is important that you have made a firm decision to change. A decision to do one thing eliminates something else. For example, if you want to quit smoking you have to first make a decision to "be" a non-smoker! Once that decision is made, that eliminates the decision to smoke. You can't be a smoker and a non-smoker at the same time. You can't make both decisions at the same time. You might say, "Well I am tapering off and smoking less and less." Well, you are still a smoker. You have made a decision to still smoke. You are one or the other… fat or skinny, healthy or non-healthy, wealthy or not, drug user or not. Whatever it is you want is not a decision to "give it a try," but a decision to go all the way!

The next step is taking action toward what you want. And when you do, you must realize that every action you take from this point forward is either moving you in the direction of your desired outcome or away from it. There is no middle ground. You want to lose weight but you still stop at McDonalds for the Big Mac for lunch, simply means you need to re-evaluate your decision. There is no right and wrong here. It just is what it is.

Also realize that in order to get something different in your life, you must do something in a different way, and that will require you stepping out of your comfort zone. Anything, anything you want lies just one step in the right direction... just taking one small step at a time, and possibly an uncomfortable step, until you reach your desired outcome.

When you take steps to change, you'll be faced with discomfort, fears and doubt. In fact, changing can bring up your deepest fears... fears of failing, "What if I can't do this? What if it doesn't work? What will others think of me? I tried before and failed. What if I can't do it this time?" The list goes on and on. It can even bring up the fear of success... "What if I'm successful? Will I have to change? Can I handle the change? Will I be okay without this crutch?" And trust me it is a crutch, and you'll be attached to it for life unless you decide to let it go and do something in a different way than you've done in the past. Change requires that you change. It's a battle between the old you and the new you you want to become."

To overcome seemingly insurmountable obstacles you have to be willing to endure some pain of change. Along with that you have to be bold. You have to stand by your decision and not let the mind chatter pull you down. Change can be like free falling out of an airplane... it's both exhilarating and scary at the same time.

Remember that the "you" that is reading this book can't accomplish those things you want. In order to have those things, you have to become a different "you." If you attempt to change using the same old thoughts and behaviors that you've always used, you'll end up with the same old results.

Whatever you're feeling... depression, anger, fear or anxiety, as it comes up remember that it is just energy wanting to be released and you are in complete control. As you feel it, stop for a moment and observe your feeling and then ask yourself these questions:

"Do I like feeling this way?" If your answer is "no" move to the next question.

"Will honoring this feeling take me in the direction I want to go?" If your answer is "no" move to the next question.

"Do I want to let it go?" If your answer is "yes" move to the next question.

"Am I willing to let it go?" If your answer is "yes" then move to the last question.

"When…When will I let it go?

And your answer should be apparent… NOW!

By the time you get to the last question you'll discover that the feeling has left you. It may come back but you have advanced to the next level. With each release the feelings get weaker and less frequent.

Hanging on requires a tremendous amount of energy, sometimes all your energy, and it will get you nowhere except more of the same. Letting go, on the other hand, requires no energy at all. It's simply a choice!

The last and most important thing is to love yourself above all else. Any feeling that is not loving toward yourself or others is based in fear. Darkness is the absence of light, just like fear is the "feeling" of the absence of love.

One of the most basic fears we have about letting go is the fear of the emptiness we believe will be there when we do. But in reality, when we die to the old, a vacuum is created for the new. That empty space is instantly filled with love. When we simply surrender a fear, the vacuum is then filled with love, and it happens without any effort whatsoever.

If you become an observer of your emotions… really observe them, you will no longer be attached to them. You can just allow them to "be there" without acting on them. You will eventually come to the realization that the origin of suffering can be put aside and can be let go of.

Letting go simply means that you leave emotions as they are. What you pay attention to grows in strength. What you don't pay attention to withers away from lack of attention. It does not mean that they are gone forever, even though some might be. It is more like observing and letting them be. Through the practice of letting go you'll begin to realize that hanging on to outdated experiences, feelings, and emotions is the origin of suffering and conflict. All conflict is self-conflict.

When you find yourself attached, look at it this way. If I'm holding onto this book and I set it down on the table, I have let it go. Just because you have the book doesn't mean you have to carry it with you day after day for the rest of your life. The book is not the problem, just like the emotional suffering is not the problem. The problem is hanging on to it. So what do you do? Let it go, lay it aside. You simply put it down gently without any kind of conflict, just like putting the book on the table and walking away.

You can apply this insight to letting go of a fear, anger, anxiety or any other self-conflict. So when you are feeling inner conflict, the moment that you refuse to indulge in that feeling is letting go.

We all have moments when everything we do seems to work. It is during these times that great insights occur. We feel abundant, happy, and trusting of life. We are refreshingly still inside, our usual nagging "chatter" is quiet, and our energy flow is profoundly open. In this state we are able to experience our own true nature, love, and the full beauty of our surroundings. We feel alive, balanced and purposeful. Then suddenly, without any notice at all, this vibrant, loving state disappears as mysteriously as it came. Our soaring spirits seems to fall back to sleep, as we drift back into our old identity. We begin to once again "buy into" the illusionary, self-created tensions of worry, fear, depression, anxiety and scarcity, which restrict us from being in the moment and living the life we want.

Any feeling that is not loving toward yourself or others is based in fear. When you let go of fear all you have left is love. Love truly has no opposite. It is an energy that travels so fast that it's everywhere at once. Even in your most dark moments love is always present. In fact love is presenting you with the fear saying "If you let go of this, you can have more of me."

We have some misconceptions about love, however. The first is that it comes from outside us, and the second is that it is secured through relationships. If we narrow love down to these two things, we are cheating ourselves out of the endless possibilities that exist. Love is always present inside us. It's just that we've disconnected by buying into our fears.

The depth of connection you feel becomes stronger as you let go of the fear, doubt, anger, blame, etc. Love is the spirit that lives within each of us.

One of the most basic fears we have about letting go, is the fear of the emptiness we believe will be there when we do. But in reality, when you die to the old, a vacuum is created for the new. That empty space is instantly filled with love. When you simply surrender a false belief, a fear, the vacuum is then filled with love, and it happens without any effort whatsoever.

You'll begin to see that every seemingly painful event is truly a gift designed to show us the power of love if we'll just let go and embrace it. Remember: What you pursue will always elude you. What you become is what you'll create. If you pursue love, it will always be "out there" somewhere, in the next relationship, job, or outside event. When you love yourself, you'll begin to discover love in everything you do, and in everyone you meet.

Receiving comes first, then giving. And what you give to others, you also give to yourself.

And of course the reverse is also true: What you withhold from yourself, you withhold from others, and again from yourself.

Letting go is essential in living a balanced life. Too much focus in one area of your life can literally suck the energy and life out of another area. When you are in balance, energy flows as it should."

The Change

JIM LUTES

Say the name Jim Lutes and chances are a top performer in your company has attended one or more of his dynamic trainings over the last few years.

Having taught his branded form of human performance since the early 1990s, Mr. Lutes has accelerated top level entrepreneurs throughout his career by conducting trainings on personal growth and subconscious programming into worldwide markets.

During this time Jim took his skills regarding the human mind, and combining it with trainings on influence, persuasion and communication strategies, he launched Lutes International in the early 1990s. Based in *San Diego California*, Jim has taught seminars for corporations, sales forces, individuals and athletes. Having appeared on television, radio and worldwide stages, Jim's style, knowledge and effectiveness provide profound results.

"Jim Lutes possesses a unique ability to create performance change in an individual in a fraction of the time it takes his competitors." The core of humans decisions are based on the programs we acquire, reinforce and grow. Combining Jim's various trainings, individuals can reach new levels of achievement and fulfillment in all areas of life. The results are at times nothing short of astonishing.

"My goal is to take that embryonic greatness that exists inside every person in America, foster it, empower it, and then hand them personal strategies based on solid principles that allow them to take that new attitude and apply it to creating a life by design."

CREATING YOUR LIFE MASTERPIECE

By Jim Lutes

Most people think that if they can just learn enough, earn enough, get smart enough, then they will BE enough. And they think that when that happens they can finally relax and be happy. But what happens is that they get so caught up in what they are constantly *doing* that they are not focused on how they are *being*.

In other words, they are not focused on their emotional state. When you engage your emotions, your subconscious mind begins to get the messages and begins to establish new rules and new behaviors. It then becomes a way of life and enters your heart, and really begins to come from your heart. When it is in your heart, then it is truly part of you. When you are really getting it at the deepest level, when you can begin to anticipate what I am going to say, you know you understand it at a much deeper level right now.

I began to study human performance as a way to make some changes in my own life and when I began to see some serious results, I got so excited about it that I wanted to share it with other people. And so I committed my life to learning and sharing what works with others. So, I am a committed lifetime learner and therefore I have been fortunate enough to have had the ability to look at and study just about every approach there is to personal development and success that is available in today's market. I am a strong advocate of clear, simple, workable approaches that get dependable and lasting results.

Because of the vast wealth of information my Life Masterpiece teaching gives people, and the amazing results they get, it is often they'll find themselves returning to it again and again throughout their life.

No matter how successful we are, or how successful we become, we all need a coach to encourage us, to challenge us, to remind us to live up to our potential.

Let's get started now.

That person that you are and that person that you must become in order to put the colors of your life masterpiece where you want them, and blend them in just the right combination to create your own unique experience, might right now seem like two very different people, but they are one in the same. You are that person right now. I am going to help you uncover your true identity and purpose so that you can then activate the universal laws and make them work for you.

When we let go of all the stories we have been telling ourselves about who we think we are supposed to be and what we think we are supposed to do and have, we not only free ourselves, we free our families, our children, our intimate partners, and our friends in the process. There is no way you can make a difference in yourself without touching somebody else, even if it is not your intention.

The Life Masterpiece focus is about what you can do with YOU. If you want to change any circumstance, any relationship, then you must begin with yourself no matter how convinced you are that somebody else or something else must change. Changing yourself can change even the most rigid system and stubborn person. And ANY progress moves you forward. And any movement forward on your part creates the opportunity for every other part of your life to be moved forward as well.

One of the most effective ways for you to reprogram your mind is through what I like to call vicarious experiences. These are the experiences other people have had, and I will bring you through their experiences by sharing their stories with you. These stories are not in this book simply to fill it up and make it fat like you find in some books. These stories are the heart and soul of the book because this is how you will begin to reprogram your subconscious and take the information into your heart where it will transform you.

The reason why vicarious experiences are so powerful is because they relate to you; and so when you are reading these stories, your conscious mind will let go and your unconscious mind will get the lesson.

When you read some of these remarkable stories and meet some of these people who have gone through some amazing personal transformations, you will begin to realize that no matter who you are, no matter what part of the world you are from or what culture you grew up in, whether you grow up poor, wealthy or somewhere in between, whether you grow up with religion or Monday Night Football, you will begin to realize that we all have the same problems.

So what will happen is you will begin to connect with these people because they have the same problems you have - the same challenges. They are universal. And you will learn that the reason for this is that we all have the same basic needs and our lives are about meeting these needs; and that they impact and determine every single thing we do and every decision we make. Every single habit, behavior, rule or pattern, is your unconscious way of trying to get your needs met. And your needs are the same exact needs every other human being on the planet has. We all use different behaviors to get these needs met, but they are still the same.

Some of the behaviors we use are positive and healthy and some of them are not quite so resourceful. And this is one of the reasons why even though we all have the same needs and the same problems, we all get different results. We are hard-wired with the same needs, but not with the same subconscious programming. And the reason why we all get different results boils down to one thing- standards.

You know, so often in life, we find ourselves in a position where we live life a certain way. We act a certain way. We were raised a certain way. And through our lives in an effort to avoid pain and still meet our needs, we made critical decisions about who we are and how we think we need to be. And so we believe we know who we are.

But the way we have behaved for years is simply an *adaptation*. Something that happened in response to the desire we had to meet our basic needs - to get the love, or respect, or acceptance from a parent, lover, loved one or peers - caused us to make a key decision and adapt to the circumstances around us. We do not ever realize that for years we have been living something that we are really good at but which is not necessarily our true nature.

One of the things you will learn here is that a single decision has the power to change everything in a heartbeat. In fact, while you stay with the process, you are going to learn about decisions you have made, perhaps some time ago, that have determined the choices you have made in the course of your life up until now. Today, you've made a decision to pick up this book and begin this journey. And this decision might be the decision that changes everything in your life from today on.

Now that you've made the decision to read it, I will tell you what this book can really do for you. It will get you to uncover, and maybe for the first time really identify, how the role models of your life have affected your subconscious decision-making in ways you never dreamed possible.

Without getting into the actual science behind it, a child's brain works much differently than an adult brain. As you might already know, our brains operate using four different wavelengths - Alpha, Beta, Theta and Delta. Most of the time, the adult brain operates at the beta level when we are awake. The beta level is when our eyes are focused in our conscious mind is in control, and we are logical. The alpha level is a level that we must pass through to go to sleep and to wake up, and it's also the most common level as when we are in a trance. Theta is for a deeper trance or dreaming, and Delta is for deep sleep. This means that when we are at the alpha level, we are highly impressionable, because the messages are going directly into our subconscious minds. A child's mind is different because it operates primarily at the alpha level, which is why children are so impressionable. This also means that our parents and other significant people in our childhood had a tremendous impact on the messages that are subconscious mind received and events from our childhood had a strong impact on our self-image, our identity, and how we develop as adults. This is why when we speak about reprogramming the subconscious mind, it is very important to talk about childhood and relationship with parents. This is not done to point fingers or place blame, but to help us understand some of the reasons for the choices that we make, for the patterns that we keep repeating, and how they carry over from generation to generation.

Even if you feel like you held your own when you were growing up, and that the relationships that you had as a child - especially the relationship you had with your mother and father - were strong, and you feel like you are strong as a result, there are still patterns that your subconscious mind is running that no longer serve you. Because it's the tension, the experience of having to deal with all of the events of your past - and even the events that happened before you were born, in your parent's past - all of these experiences affect your decision making, your relationships, your finances, your choices, behaviors and life circumstances, even today.

Even if your childhood was perfect and you feel like you honor, respect and love your parents and adore all of your siblings, and even if your parents are your greatest role models, you are still affected on many levels and in many ways. And because you decided to read this book, I believe you have some things you would like to change. If you change anything, first you must learn to reprogram your subconscious mind; and part of doing so is to understand that the key decisions you made in the past still impact you today.

Our childhood role models deeply affect both our conscious and subconscious decision-making and behavior patterns. We are all examples, and some of us are warnings. We all, at one time or another, impact other people. This is one of the reasons why I stress that it is so important to live consciously, and be an example.

When I ask people about their belief systems, and the habits and patterns that basically control their lives, I am often struck by how few of these beliefs and habits were ever chosen by that person on a conscious level. In other words, the rules that are guiding your life about how to BE in your own life very often were picked up unconsciously.

It is incredible how common it is that people start this process. When they begin to reassess their lives and their relationships with themselves and others in the success they are having or perhaps not having, they discover that much of what has been screwing up their lives, their achievements, their finances, their careers, their intimate relationships, and even their bodies, (and I am not talking about the excuse many of us use about genetics being the reason our bodies look the way they do) was influenced by their PARENTS. Not by their parents problems necessarily, but by somehow trying to be liked, loved or appreciated by one parent. Many times these decisions also have to do with trying to avoid pain that was inflicted by a parent or other significant role model, or simply standing up to a parent.

We can be 40, 50, even 80 years old, and we are still living the strategies of a child.

And what's even worse, is that very often when we were a kid, we said, "I'll never be like that!" And here you are today, exactly like that! You don't want to admit it but if you held up a mirror and watched a film of your interactions you would say, "Oh my God, I never wanted to be like that parent." And yet you are. Or perhaps you have done the opposite. Perhaps you have thrown the pendulum the other way and you're not like that parent at all. Now, you are something worse. Or, let's just say you are something else. You are the opposite of the extreme you didn't like. And so now you are another extreme. That doesn't work either. Because no one teaches us this stuff, and so it becomes unconscious. We don't even see it. It's part of the invisible fabric of our thinking and decision-making every single day.

Give yourself a unique opportunity to look deep inside yourself. It will allow you to look inside of your relationships, your decisions about money, and your decisions about your career, your relationship with God or your higher power, and even your body. It will allow you to understand how your own upbringing has maybe influenced you - and you probably know a lot of the ways it has influenced you - but maybe you'll spot some of the decisions you have made, maybe even one core decision that has affected your identity.

So, what the heck does identity mean anyway? It can be such a big and often loaded word. Well, I believe identity is the strongest force in the human personality. If you want to know what shapes you the most it's not your capability. It's your identity and the rules you have for who you think you are.

And you know what the challenge is? Most of us defined ourselves a long time ago. And when we step outside that definition, we get really uncomfortable, because the strongest force in the human personality is the need to remain consistent with how we define ourselves. Later, we will talk about the human needs as referred to earlier. One of them is certainty. What this means is that if certainty is one of the deepest needs we have, then if you don't know who you are, you do not know how to act.

Very early in life, we begin to define who we are. We use labels such as loner, aggressive, conservative, sexy, successful, loser, rich, poor, in charge. I work for others. I am ugly. I am smart. I am a procrastinator. I am clumsy. I am athletic. I am thin. I am big boned. What happens is these definitions become self-fulfilling prophecies, because nobody wants to be disappointed. Nobody wants to live in a place of uncertainty. So there may be arranging your identity or in your definition of yourself, but it may not be absolute.

The metaphor that you so often hear of when we talk about our comfort zone, is that our comfort zone is like a thermostat. We all have our comfort zone, and it is set by our subconscious mind. So if your subconscious mind has set your thermostat in a particular area of your life, for example, how much money you make, that let's say 45°, and if the temperature drops down to 40°, guess what happens? It doesn't meet your identity. In other words, things are not good enough, whether it be mentally and emotionally financially with your weight (which by the way is the primary reason people who lose weight tend to gain it back because they lose it before reprogramming their subconscious mind to reset the thermostat) or whatever.

So if you drop down to 40° in your finances and 45° is your identity, this means that 45° is what you must have. Or, if you drop down to 70° in your intimacy and 80° is your identity, then this is what you must have. Whatever it is, when you drop below your comfort zone, you will be compelled to drive to make it better automatically. If your body gets out of control, there is a point at which you go, "that's enough!" You are willing to be a little off your identity but not that much. And suddenly you go on the diet suddenly make the change because you feel the pressure that comes with being inconsistent with your own definition of how you think you should be.

But what most of us fail to recognize is that this happens on the other side as well. Your subconscious mind sets your mental thermostat at say 45° for your finances or 80° mentally for how close you want to be with your intimate partner, or 70° for how your body should look and feel.

This is not your *goal*. Your goal is something much larger. This is your subconscious comfort zone or your subconscious definition of yourself. For example, you might think of yourself as big boned, but if it suddenly isn't good enough and you really become overweight, then you change to fit your self-image or your definition of yourself in order to get back into that comfort zone. But also, what if it gets better than you expected? Perhaps you lose a lot of weight and get really good shape, or perhaps you lead your company in sales for two quarters in a row when you normally come in third or fourth, or perhaps you jump from 70° in your intimacy, and now you have a relationship that is at 90° or even 100°. Maybe you have a really hot, passionate relationship with more passion than you ever have before, or you lose three dress sizes instead of one, or you double your income, whatever it is, your subconscious mind starts talking some sense into you. And your brain goes, "Hello, dude what the heck are you doing? You are 70°'er, what in heck are you doing way up here at 90°? You can't keep that. That's not going to last. Get back down to 70° before you get hurt or fail or screw it up. You're in over your head. You're not an entrepreneur. You work for other people."

Wherever your subconscious mind has set your comfort zone based on the way you define yourself, you're going to keep adjusting to stay in that comfort zone. So many times in these types of programs, people challenge you to get out of your comfort zone, which you can't do consciously. You have to go into your subconscious and reset your comfort zone, just like you would the thermostat. And this will keep happening until you reprogram your subconscious mind with a new identity, and the new comfort zone. Before you set out to make any kind of lasting change, you must reset your subconscious comfort zone.

To contact Jim:

info@lutesinternational.com

www.lutesinternational.com

www.jimluteslive.com

KASEY HIGBEE

Author, speaker, philanthropist and entrepreneur, Kasey Higbee, says, "I wish for a life lived to the fullest potential at every turn. My desire is to use my talents and resources to positively impact as many lives as I can." This has been Kasey's mission and her purpose for the past decade and every decision she makes aligns with that vision. In fact, that is why she contributed to this very book, because she knows, "The Change will be a transformative tool in thousands of lives worldwide."

Helping individuals and organizations identify their deepest desires, develop strategies to accomplish those goals, and refine the process to increase efficiency and outcomes, is Kasey passion. Currently, she is one of the leading affiliates in the world's fastest growing personal development company, Quanta. "Bottom line," Kasey says, "through Quanta, I am able to facilitate sudden and significant change in lives around the globe, while simultaneously growing my own lucrative international business. I am headed to the top and bringing as many people with me as possible. So, if my message resonates with you, and you are willing to bring your rock solid work ethic and enthusiasm to the table, then I am completely confident that my team and I can teach you the rest. Let's change the world! It's go time!"

NAY-SAYERS BE DAMNED!

By Kasey Higbee

Columbus was not void of passion when he sailed the seas and discovered America; his enthusiasm at times was perhaps the only wind in his sails. President Lincoln was not apathetic in his pursuit to abolish slavery - thank God! Tesla did not receive patents for a system of transmitting electrical energy because he was indifferent to his project. Thomas Edison didn't invent the light bulb in one fell swoop; it took perseverance. Martin Luther King's "I Have a Dream" speech is not remembered for being delivered in monotone. Neil Armstrong didn't become the first person to walk on the Moon as a result of half-heartedly training for his journey. Michael Jordan didn't make it from Brooklyn to the NBA without a passionate pursuit. Oprah didn't become the media proprietor, talk show host, actress, producer, and philanthropist we know today by way of disinterest in her own success. Think of your greatest accomplishments in life to date; were they achieved void of zest, vigor, and zeal? Not likely. Ralph Waldo Emerson put it simply, "Nothing great was ever achieved without enthusiasm."

We have within us Greatness - a limitless reservoir of Ultimate Potential, Power, and Purpose. You can call this greatness God or Source. You can attribute it to spirituality or science. I am not interested in that argument. A rose by any other name is still a rose. What matters is that right now, this incredible potential is percolating within you! So how do we unleash the potential, tap into that power and live our purpose? Well, it won't happen by accident; it takes decision and action, fueled by both serious intention and enthusiasm.

Let us start by examining the enthusiasm gurus - children. Every child has grandiose dreams of being an astronaut, the president, a pop-star, or in my brother's case, a cocker spaniel! What did you want to be when you grew up? What did you long for? When your young imagination ran wild, what adventures did you find yourself on? How many yards were you willing to mow in order to get the telescope you wanted so you could see beyond the stars? As a young child with a dream, to what lengths would you go to see that dream fulfilled? Nay-sayers be damned! To hell with the doubters, realists and critics! A child's dream is impermeable; it is protected by their enthusiasm and faith.

Envision this: a little boy who dreams of becoming a firefighter is watching television when he hears a distant siren growing closer. He jumps to his feet, smiling from ear to ear. In less than 2.2 seconds, he crosses the living room, scales the davenport, crawls under the dining-room table and smashes his doe-eyed face against the front window. He grins just to catch a glimpse of the fire engine as it passes by his house. *That* is enthusiasm!

Upon hearing the sirens, he didn't begin calculating the potential ROI of his efforts. He didn't think of the cost-benefit ratio or potential consequences of his actions. He heard the sirens calling to a deep passion in his soul and he went running.

This is not to say enthusiasm trumps due diligence. As mature adults with an understanding of cause and effect, we would be remiss to ignore the potential costs of our actions. But as we do so, we run the risk of dimming our passionate flame inside. We must walk this line with caution; vigilant in our efforts to fan the flame of excitement as we navigate the obstacles that line the path we have chosen to take.

As we age, our aspirations mature and develop, as does everything that grows. However, our enthusiasm for our dreams doesn't have to wane simply because our dreams change and grow. In fact, those who maintain youthful enthusiasm in pursuit of their mature dreams are the ones who cross the finish line first, and are still smiling ear-to-ear.

What happens then as we age, that dampens our spirit and disconnects us from this Greatness, this life-giving Source within? *We change.* We relinquish control to external forces; we buy into limiting beliefs and self-destructive patterns. Like a frog brought slowly to a boil, we allow our Greatness to escape from within us, little-by-little as the surrounding world changes. We're picked last for games at recess; we don't grasp algebra as easily as our classmates; our bodies look different than those of our peers; we have no date to prom; we don't get accepted to our first choice of college; a boyfriend or girlfriend finds us lacking and we find ourselves alone; we didn't get the job, or if we did, our boss doesn't appreciate our work; bills are overdue; the house payment is behind… and life goes on, and on, and on. Therein lies mankind's greatest tragedy: we begin to weave together a tapestry of lies about who we are, what we can accomplish, and what we are worth. Under the weight of such despair, our enthusiasm retreats to protect our egos from yet another bash.

So what do I say to this? Well, with all due respect, we need to grow up. I know it is paradoxical to encourage us to maintain youthful enthusiasm while simultaneously calling upon us all to handle failure with wisdom and maturity, but your dreams depend on your doing so! Paulo Coelho's remark rings true, "There is just one thing that makes your dream become impossible: the fear of failure." This fear of failure is real for us all, to varying degrees. The issue is not that the fear exists; rather, it is how we choose to respond to this fear that makes or breaks us.

Perhaps it is a result of the increasingly dramatic nature of mankind that, by-and-large, we perceive failure as finite - a destination rather than a detour. Herein lies another opportunity to change a limiting belief and fiercely hold onto a rather liberating truth: failure is *not* an end result, but simply the result of quitting before you're done! Consider what some of the greats have said on the subject:

> "Our greatest glory is not in never falling but in rising every time we fall." - Confucius

"I didn't fail 1,000 times. The light bulb was an invention with 1,000 steps." - Thomas Edison

"You never fail until you stop trying." - Albert Einstein

"Every strike brings me closer to the next home run." - Babe Ruth

"Success consists of going from failure to failure without loss of enthusiasm." - Winston Churchill

"I've failed over and over again in my life. That is why I succeed." - Michael Jordan

If you're awake at all, what you begin to notice about the successful people in this world is not that they *never* fail, but that despite failing *often*, they keep pressing forward. This is not a phenomenon beyond our understanding. It is quite simple; a change in mindset can take the ordinary and propel them into extraordinary. This is true for you and me alike!

From as early as I can remember, my father taught me about choice and accountability. If fingers were pointed in our home, they were only allowed to be pointed inward. These lessons were hard at times; actually painful and confusing for a hormonal female teen like me. However, with a relentless love, my father's aim was to instill within my four brothers and me an internal locus of control. No outside circumstances, events, influences, or people could determine our fate. Nor was our life to be viewed as a result of chance or random happening. We were taught that our destiny was the result of our beliefs and subsequent choices and actions. This mindset demands personal accountability and admonishes the victim mentality. This mindset encourages endurance, self-awareness, growth, and the ongoing passionate pursuit of a life lived to the fullest. This mindset fuels success.

"Okay Kasey," you think skeptically as you search for a flaw in my logic. "If a man or woman can succeed at anything they have unlimited enthusiasm for, and they understand failure is nothing more than a stepping stone, then why aren't more people wildly successful?"

To which I reply, "It is simple; the majority of us lack an acute awareness of what we want."

Remember, the little boy from my example above, who tore through the living room to see the fire truck pass by? Had he not known that he desperately wanted to be a fireman, the siren would have still sounded and he would have heard its high pitch above his television program, but would he have gone running? No. You see, if we don't know what we want, then we won't know where to focus our enthusiasm and efforts. Being blind to your desires and dreams can lead to one of two outcomes. One, you become a drone floating through life without direction. Or, like an untied helium balloon, you erratically travel throughout space and time, exerting small bursts of energy here and there, never fully arriving anywhere, until you find yourself completely deflated.

Listen. Do you want the four points of success summed up in 14 words? Here:

Figure out what you want.

Get fired up about it.

Take action.

Don't stop.

My advice, which I hope you heed, is to *not* rush through step one. The rest will follow naturally once you have a clear, precise vision of what it is you want.

As a life coach, public speaker, author, and citizen of the world, I work with students, business men and women, presidents and CEO's of multimillion dollar companies, non-profit organizations, mothers, fathers, orphans, elderly, the rich and the poor. What I have found is that no one has the exact same life dream and set of desires. More importantly, I have found that no one's dreams are less valid, less worthy of pursuit, or less honorable or attainable than anyone else's. Yet when we begin an exercise of self-discovery to align ourselves with our dreams, we often look to what other people have created, strived for, or valued. You cannot foster the enthusiasm needed nor nurture the type of perseverance required to pursue someone else's dream; you *must* create your own dream. Choose to have the courage to own that dream and do what it takes to achieve it!

For many of my clients, uncovering their life's passion and deepest desires is a matter of starting with their values. If you're open to the exercise, I invite you to partake: Go online and search for "list of values." As you read over the hundreds of values listed, choose your top 10 and order them from most important on down. Resist the temptation to create a list that your husband would like or your mother would be proud of; this is your list, your values, and it doesn't have to be approved by anyone but you. This part of the exercise might take five minutes, but for some I have seen this take five months. The length of time it takes is not important. The end result we seek is a genuine list of your top 10 values.

With that list set aside, envision all the things you want in life. It is easy to list the material things we'd like to possess (houses, cars, vacations), so start there if need be. However, also consider the intangibles. How do you physically feel? How about emotionally? What about your relationships? Who is in your life? How do they feel about you and you them? Shoot! How do you feel about yourself? Think about the daily stuff; what is your typical morning like? What does work mean to you? What do you do for a living? Who do you see daily? Some of my clients find it easy to get a quick paragraph or so jotted down, but get stuck when asked for more. If this is you, close your eyes and ask yourself to imagine every detail of your life if you lived each day void of any excuses.

Next, begin finding connections between that which you desire (your "wants") and that which you value (your "whys"). Knowing what you want is powerful; supporting that desire with an awareness of why you want it makes your pursuit indestructible. Keep your "wants" and your "whys" at the forefront of your mind. Like arrows of your mighty quiver, they are ready to be fired at any challenges that may arise. If your actions bring you closer to that which you want, do not retreat! Recite out loud your 10 values and push forward knowing that you have within you Greatness; a limitless reservoir of ultimate potential, power, and purpose. Do not fear failure. Do not fear success. If you must fear, then fear only an ambivalent life where your amazing potential is left untapped.

If you come across a road block and you just want to give up, I am willing to bet you have not truly determined what it is you want. If you had, then your enthusiasm could propel you past the obstacle and onto success. Make the change. The change is to begin relentlessly pursuing your own life, not the lives others have designed for themselves. The change is to shift from an external to an internal locus of control. The change is to know what you want intimately, not casually. The change is to not fear failure (or success), but to embrace the journey. The change is taking place within you. The change is you. The change is now.

To learn more about Kasey's work:

www.wealthwithinyourreach.com

www.networkofsuccess.com

www.LinkedIn.com/In/kaseyhigbee

omnigrateful@gmail.com

MAX HIGBEE

Dr. Max Higbee's desire is to facilitate a powerful and positive change in the dental profession, starting with you and your practice! For over 40 years he has grown his practice from dismal income to a $5 million a year practice. Most of that growth has taken place in the last 10 years and resulted from tangible duplicatable steps. Dr. Higbee feels, "Now it is time for me to take my decades of experience and pass on some of the best kept secrets in our profession to the next generation of dentist." His passion is to leave a legacy, his purpose is to transform lives and his mission is to start with you!

There is never a better time then right now to take the next step, especially when a multimillionaire dental entrepreneur is standing by, ready to mentor you along the way.

THERE IS NO SUCH THING AS SMALL CHANGE

By Max Higbee

What most would consider small change was a magnificent discovery to my mother, Ilene. Growing up in the Depression, she lived very poor throughout her childhood. Needless to say, she was always delighted when she found even a penny on the sidewalk. She knew that all money, even "small change," would grow into dollars and so she respected and valued all money, big or small. I always think of her when I bend over to pick up an abandoned penny. I am also reminded of the abundance of the universe and how blessed I am for choosing to find value in *all* that is provided, if we just choose to "pick it up." So when presented with an opportunity to "bend over and pick up" a gift from the universe, I never scoff at its size because I know - *there is no such thing as small change.*

Bringing exactly what you want into sharp focus is a change that makes all the difference in your success. Once you know where you are going, then every subsequent choice will bring you closer to that which you desire. Most people live their lives like a ship with no rudder, just floating in the changing winds. The toughest question we need to answer is: "What do I want?" Addressing that question - going from uncertainty to clarity about what you want can seem like a small change. However, with a specific destination in mind, your sails and pulleys become tools to make the most of the winds and currents.

Consider for example, the three frogs sitting on a log over a pond. One decided to jump in the water. How many frogs are then left on the log? If you said two, you are wrong. The answer is three; I said one *decided* to jump in the water. The critical distinction here is that decision does not necessarily equal action.

Decision is only the first step, just a thought or possibility. Only action, in this case jumping, can create a change. The seemingly small change, moving from decision to action makes all the difference! Seems simple enough; know what you want and take action to get there. So why do we struggle with this concept?

Humans are naturally drawn to a victim mindset because it is often the path of least resistance. We need to change this. The choice to be a victim is a losing choice which strips you of your power to create your life just as you want it. If you choose to play the game of life as an accountable player, then you are empowered with the ability to create all the outcomes for your life. This is the very foundation of any potential self-improvement and the value in it is life-altering.

For many years, my biggest obstacle was to let go of my victim mentality, and instead embrace an empowered mindset. Humor me and imagine a time in your life when you were a victim of someone or some set of circumstances. Take a few minutes and write it down with as much detail as possible. Here is mine:

> *A friend suggested we go skydiving. He felt that the experience would allow me to better cope with my fear of heights. The facility we went to was as shabby as the plane that took us up. Our entire pre-jump instructions were: jump, keep your eyes on the horizon, toes pointed down and roll when you hit the ground. We jumped with a static line that opened the chute; this was an old, World War II, round, white canopy. The wind was blowing 25 knots, with gusts up to 30. Four of us jumped, including the instructor, and three of us were injured. The instructor broke both wrists and I fractured the ball of my right femur and broke the femur itself in 17 places. They had inadequately*

> *trained us, their equipment was antiquated, and we jumped when it was way too windy. To this day, my right leg is two inches shorter and they could have prevented it all.*

That is my victim story. Do you see how easy it is to shift blame to external forces?

Now what I would like you to do is rewrite your story as if you - just you - were 100% accountable for your experience. Look how this alternative perspective changes my story:

> *I had always chosen to be afraid of heights. I read that to overcome our fears, we must use that "fear-energy" as a propellant to attack the fear and overcome it. So I chose skydiving. I didn't look into who was teaching it, how long they had been doing it, or even if they had any certification to instruct. I didn't even inquire about their safety records. I called them and made the appointment. I drove 4 hours to get to their facility, paid them and off I went. I chose to skydive. I even signed an extensive disclaimer before we went up. I jumped out of the plane. I broke my own leg, as surely as if I had laid on a railroad track in front of an oncoming train.*

Just like that, you suddenly had control of your life. Which version of your story is closer to reality for you? Would you have done something differently?

This simple exercise transformed my perspective. Regardless of the event, I always ask myself "why did I create this?" I live my life accordingly, knowing that I have a choice in everything that comes to me, or at least accountability for how I choose to feel about it. I like to ask my audiences a series of questions, and ask them to raise their hand if they agree:

> Did you choose to come to this event?
>
> Did you choose what to eat today?
>
> Did you choose to brush your teeth today?
>
> Did you choose your level of education?

Did you choose which sex to be born?

Did you choose your own parents prior to birth?

When would your hand go down? If I were in the audience, my hand would remain up for every single question because I have chosen to change from a victim mindset to a more empowered mindset; one of total accountability. If you choose to play the game of life as an accountable player, then you are in charge of creating all the outcomes for your life. This is the very foundation of any potential self-improvement.

There are countless arenas of life in which to pursue change. The same principles apply to any aspect of life:

- Answer the question "What do I want?"

- Take action on your decisions.

- Hold yourself accountable for all outcomes.

Once I became comfortable being totally accountable, I decided to eliminate all the relationships that I had allowed to diminish my energy. I choose to surround myself with genuine people who are real and exhibit good hearts, and those who weren't seemed to just fade away. I like to call it "soaring with eagles" rather than "flocking with turkeys." My productivity doubled and my stress decreased, resulting in a more joyous life. This is yet another seemingly small change that ended up having enormous value.

The truth is that we cannot know much of anything with absolute certainty, except perhaps our personal feelings; we are the indisputable expert on what we feel. If we don't choose our own feelings, then where could they possibly come from? The skydiving experience was a disaster; however, it allowed me to overcome my fear of heights. I decided to change my feelings about heights, took action to do so, was accountable to the outcomes, learned, grew, and eventually became a private pilot. This has helped me immensely in the past 20 years to obtain the total freedom to do, go, and be, wherever I want.

How about the *change* that takes place when you let go of your attachment to other people's approval of who you are and what you do? This change is not a personality overhaul, it is a small decision that, when acted upon, has far reaching implications. I'm as guilty as the next person for needing the approval of others before I act, so I can testify that this mindset can paralyze an otherwise adventurous and entrepreneurial person. Choosing to change that belief, by letting go of being an "approval suck," has allowed me to live life rooted in what I believe, want, or intuit. This is a lot more fun and a lot less stressful than the alternative. If this sounds like you, experiment with some personal choices, act on them without seeking approval… the change is liberating!

These principles hold true in business too. Consider this analogy: If you place a goldfish in a mason jar, that goldfish will only grow to a size appropriate for that jar. If you change the size of the jar, let's say you put that same fish into a five gallon bucket, the goldfish will grow beyond the limits of it original home in the mason jar. Looking back, I see how this principle applies to my success in business. The same 1,100 square foot dental office I built 40 years ago has been remodeled four times to its present 11,000 square feet. With each incremental increase in the size of the building, I experienced an even larger growth in the practice's production. Bottom line, I believe a business grows to fill the size of the vision you hold. For me, my vision required a larger office space, and each time I built upon that space, my business grew. I kept enlarging my building; not because I wanted a bigger facility, but because I wanted the freedom to live as I choose. Not needing the approval of anyone else to do so was critical.

Today, my dental office produces in the top 5% of all my colleagues. More important than the income, I love my work, my staff, my clients and my family. This success was a result of seemingly "*small changes*" along the way that made all the difference. One of those changes was a change in my mindset. I used to believe that most people would take advantage of me if they could; I had high fear, with low trust. I read somewhere that 94% of people want to do the right thing by you, leaving only 6% as "bad guys". The wonderful thing is that half of that 6% are in jail! Why let 3% of the population determine how you operate? With this realization, I made a *change* and I now live with high trust and low fear. In 2011, I chose to give my personal cell phone number to each of my 8000+ clients. I had to give up my fear that those people would bombard my personal space. My personal space is intact and my business grew tremendously with people who value having personal access when they really need it. Yet again, a small change with huge results.

Twenty years ago, I changed my practice from cash-only to an office that extends credit to everyone. Now, extending credit is a risky business, especially if you want to collect 100%, which I assume is why so few of my colleagues extend credit. We are extending credit using established banking principles and fostering high trust relationships with our patients. We obtain a credit score for anyone wishing to carry a balance. We apply that score to a credit matrix that predicts 95% collection results for a given amount over a certain time period. We charge 6% interest if it is an automatic checking withdrawal; 12% if normally billed. If you stick to the well-established banking principles, your losses are minimal and your win is huge! This simple change tripled my case acceptance and generates ample interest income. Simultaneously, extending credit has had the single biggest marketing impact of any decision I have ever made.

Change is inevitable; nothing stays the same. We are either growing or shrinking. Sometimes growth involves letting go of an ill-conceived belief system. This is where I have found my greatest wins: collections. I chose to give it up; it is typically a negative, awful experience for all concerned. Plus if only 3% of the population is out to get you, you're likely going to lose only 3%... so what? If 120 days pass in my office, rather than sending them to collections, I chose to send a letter that says:

> *"Your bill of so many dollars has not been paid and we haven't heard from you. I believe you would pay us if you could and we would welcome a payment in the future, but we won't continue to bill you. We are hoping things get better for you.*
>
> *Sincerely,*
>
> *Max"*

This decision to send the "forgiving letter" is a case-by-case decision, but is what I do with about 90% of delinquent accounts. I made this change 5 years ago and my write-off percentage is no greater than it was before. In fact, many of these clients have paid their past bill, continue seeing us, and refer friends and family all the time. Payment of past debt is usually not a requirement to continue using our services. However, those whose debts have once been relieved are cash-only patients in the future, because I don't want to put them in that position again. The results of this approach have been remarkable. Yet again, a small change led to wonderful outcomes.

Every journey begins with the choice to take the first step. The journey is quicker if each step is in the direction of what you really want. Constant examination of my belief systems has helped me to make these changes, one at a time, like picking up a penny on the sidewalk. The summation is a wealth far beyond money and possessions. I encourage you to examine your beliefs and ask yourself, "Why do I believe this? Did I read it? Did I inherit it from my parents or dream it up?" More importantly, ask yourself, "Does this belief align with my values? Can holding this belief bring me closer to what I really want?" Most of us need to purge our beliefs that hold us back from being and having all that is possible. Some of the most common limiting thoughts include: I am too old, too fat, too stupid, so unlucky, so undeserving, lacking in talent, education, charisma, etc.

I achieved all of my material wants but I still felt a great void in my life. Maybe, my belief in wanting more stuff was getting in the way of what I really wanted. I found myself wondering if my life made a difference. A friend suggested it might be enlightening to write my own obituary. You know the one you hope someone writes for the paper, right after the funeral where everyone wept, for the world was a better place with you in it.

I wrote that obituary. There was not a mention of my huge house and land, the successful businesses, the airplanes and cars. Not one mention of all the countries I've seen, not a word about cutting-horses, snow-skiing or scuba diving. Instead, it mentioned all the children I have loved and raised, my wonderful wife who supported and encouraged me. There were wonderful words of praise, respect, and gratitude from friends, family, staff and clients. This was a huge paradigm shift for me; a realization that I had achieved my desires, and over time, what I want has evolved into something greater than before. A revitalization, a newness surrounded me. I was re-fired instead of retired. It was time to reexamine my values and beliefs and align with new coordinates to set my sail for the new port of what I want *now*! All of this change and internal excitement from a simple exercise of writing my own obituary.

Earl Nightingale said, "What you can see and believe, you can achieve." This has worked for me and keeps on proving true! I have seen it work for hundreds of people. I know it can work for you as well.

Be grateful for change. Remember that every change has immeasurable value. Even what seems to be the small changes have within them the potential to unlock the doors to your biggest dreams and desires. In a life lived to the fullest, there is no such thing as small change!

Learn more about Max's Dental Practice! See the guru in action and learn all you can. Healthcare providers, students, and entrepreneurs welcome!

541-548-8175

www.redmonddentalgroup.com

Redmond Dental Group

1765 Parkway Drive; Redmond, Oregon 97756

Reach out to Max for private consulting, shadowing opportunities, coaching calls, to attend a live presentation or request he present at your event (CE presentations available).

541-279-1590

www.MaxWHigbee.com

2360 Corporate Circle Suite 400; Henderson, Nevada 89074

The Change

TERRY MORGESON

Terry Morgeson is an entrepreneur with a background in aerospace and marketing. She has held a lifelong interest in nutrition and wellness and is dedicated to educating others on ways they can live a healthier, happier lifestyle. She firmly believes in getting to the root cause of issues for more effective, concrete solutions and prefers to take a natural, holistic approach to solving her health concerns.

Over the years, many people have fondly anointed her as their health guru, a mantle she proudly wears for them. She also enjoys learning about different foods and freely experiments on her family with vegetarian, paleo and gluten-free recipes, much to her son's chagrin. Her husband tells everyone that their dog eats just as healthy as the family does since she makes the dog's food from scratch as well.

An artisan at heart, Terry greatly appreciates natural living. She enjoys making body care and cleaning products such as soaps, deodorants, cleaners, laundry detergent, skin scrubs and lotions. And when she's not dazzling her family with her accomplishment, she's cheering as the #1 fan of her rock star son and his aspiring band.

Terry also comments and blogs on all things health, wellness and nutrition-related for Your Health 4 Life. You can follow her on Twitter and Instagram by searching for "terrymorgeson".

YOUR HEALTH IS A GIFT. DISEASE IS SOMETHING YOU EARN.

By Terry Morgeson

Have you ever found yourself looking at fit, healthy people and thought, "Just how do they do it?" Have you looked at them with disdain, furious that they have been so blessed? I certainly have.

If you're like me, the above might sound familiar. You've probably been guilty of self-defeating talk at times due to anger, frustration, or lack of motivation. You want to eat healthy and have a healthy body and lifestyle but it seems unachievable due to time, money, or health concerns. You may have tried every diet known but your weight returns with a vengeance. Or, perhaps the weight stays off but you struggle with chronic health complaints. You resort to negative blanket statements about others' success so you don't have to face failure. You say things you likely don't mean to protect your feelings, justifying, "That's just the way it is."

This negative self-talk is an excuse that prevents us from achieving our goals. So why would we say things that take away our power, keeping us in stasis? We claim we want change but change is scary and uncomfortable. We don't tend to make changes when we're comfortable. Can you recall the last time you experienced growth when you were comfortable?

My grandfather always told me that you have everything so long as you have your health. Wise words. Unfortunately, I still learned – the hard way – what happens when one becomes complacent. For years, I had taken my thin build and health for granted. However, weight crept up slowly; as did achy hips, allergies, thinning hair, and facial redness. Four to five hours of restless tossing became my nightly sleep routine. I got by on convenience foods and coffee. I attributed my body's changes to aging and my busy life. I was uncomfortable and wanted my body back. Yet not uncomfortable enough, otherwise I would have made a change.

My body was talking but I wasn't listening. I was busy working, running a side business and raising a family. So I ignored the signs. By the time I resumed working out, my hips stopped me. Each diet I tried worked but the weight always came back. I began to abandon hope of regaining a healthy weight or physical fitness.

After seven years of living on this roller coaster, there was suddenly a noticeable change. My face broke out in painful acne, something that had never happened to me, even as a teen. My intense hip pain made my movements comparable to that of an elderly person. My body had gained my full attention.

Initially, my dermatologist treated me with antibiotics. While they helped, I soon realized this was only a band-aid. I needed a real solution. I then visited a naturopath for blood work where I learned my adrenals were taxed, explaining my chronic exhaustion. I also discovered that I had developed a host of food allergies and was dealing with severe inflammation due to the foods I ate. I needed to make immediate changes. It was either that or take dangerous pharmaceuticals that would likely cause more problems, leading me to pay the ultimate price.

How could all these problems have arisen simply from eating certain foods? My doctor explained that my body had actually developed allergies to many of the foods I was eating due to my chronic exposure to them. I no longer digested them normally and I was deprived of nutrition. She instructed me on which foods to eliminate and which supplements would balance my nutritional deficit.

She helped me see that this didn't just "happen" to me. I had unknowingly caused these problems myself. My health was now priority one.

At first it was daunting, leaving me completely overwhelmed. I wanted this fixed but feared another failure. But as I learned more about what was happening I found that I didn't have to make all these changes overnight. In fact, this was simply a process that required time and dedication. I treated it as my newest life goal, realizing that with a little research, proper mindset, and steady, consistent progress, that I could achieve the healthy lifestyle I desired. And restore my health.

So why does healthy eating escape many of us when we have experts at the American Heart Association and MyPyramind.gov guiding us? The Harvard School of Public Health says it's because those guidelines fall short in providing nutritional advice that promotes health while reducing risk for chronic diseases[1]. Simply put, what we've been taught our entire lives about healthy eating is outdated and inaccurate.

This lack of knowledge leads to dangerous results. The *National Vital Statistics Reports* confirms that the leading causes of American deaths included heart disease, cancer, stroke, Alzheimer's, diabetes and autoimmune diseases[2]. When I looked into their root causes, I noticed inflammation was a commonality. I became thankful to have caught my concerns before they became too serious.

Inflammation is actually an essential part of the body's natural immune response. For example, when you roll your ankle, you experience an acute, regional inflammation in the form of redness, swelling, heat and pain. Your white blood cells then rush in, removing infection and damaged tissues. Anti-inflammatory agents then bring about healing and inflammation's job is complete.

---

[1] School of Public Health, Harvard. "Food Pyramids and Plates: What Should You Really Eat?" N p, n d. Web. 29 Jul. 2014. http://www.hsph.harvard.edu/nutritionsource/pyramid-full-story.
[2] U.S. Department of Health and Human Services. "National Vital Statistics Reports." *Centers for Disease Control and Prevention*, 29 May 2014. Web. 19 Jul. 2014. http://www.cdc.gov/nchs/products/nvsr.htm and http://www.cdc.gov/nchs/data/nvsr/nvsr61/nvsr61_06.pdf.

But many of us live with chronic inflammation caused by every-day stresses. You may recall having learned in school about the "fight or flight response," which is due to physiological reactions to what is perceived as harmful events or threats. This evolutionary trait protected us from nature's predators as we grew as a species. However, today we have different types of predators for which nature did not prepare us. Our bodies are constantly bombarded by toxins due to pollution, pesticides, refined, pasteurized and processed foods and genetically modified "GMO" foods known as "Frankenfoods." Our bodies wage a constant battle resulting in stress that leads many to develop sensitivities and allergic reactions to foods including sugars, dairy, and gluten.

Few of us think twice about what we consume. This coupled with changes in the quality of our foods places a constant burden on our physical and mental health. Research from the College of Natural Sciences[3] and the *Journal of the American College of Nutrition*[4] concluded that phytonutrients, which are geared to nourish us at the cellular level, are measurably lower today than in previous generations[5]. The findings show this is largely due to the manipulating of crop varieties for higher yields and increased pest resistances. There has also been a marked reduction in crop rotation which is essential to maintaining the critical balance of organic matter, nutrients, and microorganisms necessary for healthy soils.

The way our foods are grown is equally important. A June 2014 study published in the *British Journal of Nutrition* states that organic crops contain substantially higher concentrations of antioxidants. These antioxidants reduce the risk of chronic neurodegenerative diseases, and even some cancers. The study found that by switching to an organic diet, one would

---

[3] College of Natural Sciences, The University of Texas at Austin. "Study Suggests Nutrient Decline in Garden Crops Over Past 50 Years." N.p., n.d. Web. 29 Jul. 2014. http://www.utexas.edu/news/2004/12/01/nr_chemistry.

[4] Davis, MD, Donald, Melvin Epp, and Hugh Riordan. "Changes in USDA Food Composition Data for 43 Garden Crops, 1950 to 1999." *Journal of the American College of Nutrition* 2004 Dec;23(6):669-82 (2004): U.S. National Library of Medicine/National Institutes of Health/PubMed.gov. Web. 10 Aug. 2014. http://www.ncbi.nlm.nih.gov/pubmed/15637215.

[5] EarthTalk® by Roddy Scheer and Doug Moss. "Dirt Poor: Have Fruits and Vegetables Become Less Nutritious?" *Scientific American Global RSS*. N.p., n.d. Web. 10 Jul. 2014. http://www.scientificamerican.com/article/soil-depletion-and-nutrition-loss.

consume 20-40% more antioxidants without needing to consume more food or calories. The study also determined that conventionally grown crops were four times more likely to contain pesticide residues and higher concentrations of the toxic metal Cadmium.[6]

Our declining health shouldn't come as a surprise. The best foods for us to consume now only contain a fraction of the nutrients they once did. To add to the problem, we then eat less of them due to our rushed lives, relying primarily on the empty calories of processed foods. Our energy plummets, followed by mental stress, fatigue, and irritability. Inflammation recognizes our stress and rushes to protect but the stress cycle repeats. The body is confused and continues its fight response, creating more inflammation. Over time, this inflammatory response can create autoimmune or other diseases. Our bodies start turning on us. This is the cost of convenience.

Look around and you will notice not only adults but also children exhibit outward signs of inflammation, including redness, swelling, heat, stiffness, and pain. Entire countries that have adopted our Western diet now show these identical symptoms. As we lose vital nutrients we set the stage for chronic disease. It's no wonder the number of overweight and obese people is far greater today than 50 years ago and the incidence of disease is skyrocketing.

We may not be entirely to blame. We simply don't have a key understanding of nutrition. If we did we'd see that it's actually easier to achieve and maintain our health than we imagine. And we can make changes today. As Hippocrates once said, "Let food be thy medicine and medicine be thy food." It's easy to change your eating habits if you think of this as a

---

[6] Marcin Barańskia, Dominika Średnicka-Tober, Nikolaos Volakakis, Chris Seal, Roy Sanderson, Gavin B. Stewart, Charles Benbrook, Bruno Biavati, Emilia Markellou, Charilaos Giotis, Joanna Gromadzka-Ostrowska, Ewa Rembiałkowska, Krystyna Skwarło-Sońta, Raija Tahvonen, Dagmar Janovská, Urs Niggli, Philippe Nicot and Carlo Leifert. "Higher Antioxidant and Lower Cadmium Concentrations and Lower Incidence of Pesticide Residues in Organically Grown Crops: A Systematic Literature Review and Meta-Analyses." *British Journal of Nutrition: FirstView*. Volume Unknown. (26, June 2014): pp 1-18. Print.
http://journals.cambridge.org/action/displayAbstract?fromPage=online&aid=9289221&fulltextType=RA&fileId=S0007114514001366

lifestyle. Become more selective in what you eat to nourish your body. It only takes a moment to ask, "Is this good for me?" before eating.

Two of the simplest ways you can begin your journey are increasing daily hydration and scheduling regular exercise. You can replace processed and refined foods with whole foods and include grass-fed meats and raw dairy to your diet. You can also eat smaller, more frequent meals and become more mindful of your body's reactions to foods. All of which are easy.

Most of us underestimate the role proper hydration plays in our health. We forget our bodies are almost 65% water and that water is crucial to organ and muscle function. It also flushes toxins, improves complexion, maintains regularity, boosts immunity, increases energy and relieves fatigue. A general guideline for men is three liters daily and for women, two liters daily. Keeping a water bottle nearby becomes a reminder to drink up. And while it increases restroom visits, this is a good thing. Studies show we are too sedentary and need to get up and move. And don't say you have no time for exercise: A 15-minute lunch hour walk will translate to pounds in no time. Just remember to refill your bottle before returning!

The next important step is to remove highly processed and refined foods from your diet. In general, think of processed foods as anything prepackaged. Highly processed foods include lunch meat, microwavable meals, and anything jarred, canned, or bottled. They contain a multitude of unpronounceable ingredients and fillers. Minimally processed foods include bagged spinach, roasted nuts or frozen fruits and have fewer additives.

Refined foods are assassins. In exchange for extended product shelf life we lose vital dietary fiber, vitamins, and minerals. Refined foods are also laden with hidden salts, fats, and sugars, making them higher in calories yet lower in nutrients. They also tend to spike blood sugars, quickly followed by a crash, leading us to consume more. Neal Barnard, M.D. has done extensive cravings research and asserts we aren't weak-willed. Rather, the sugars in these foods release opiate-like substances that keep us hooked[7]. Their names include high-fructose corn syrup, maltose, sucrose and dextrose.

---

[7] *Chocolate, Cheese, Meat, and Sugar – Physically Addictive*. Dir. VegSource. Perf. Neal Barnard,

Start reading the labels of packaged foods for key ingredients and flavors you like. Why purchase spaghetti sauce when you can make it fresh at home while controlling additives, with only tomatoes, herbs, and oil? You can also better manage your blood sugar level by saying no to white rice or pasta and opting for brown instead. You can purchase minimally processed foods such as precut organic vegetables until you adjust to preparing everything yourself. These simple changes fit easily into a busy lifestyle. By simply replacing one home cooked meal a week, your daily habit will soon grow into a lifestyle. Before long there will be a permanent detour past those middle grocery aisles.

Another step is to eat nutrient-dense, raw, whole and organic foods and grass-fed meats. Adding nutrient-rich foods is crucial to fueling our cells' mitochondria, the mini cellular powerhouses that manage our energy supply. Our mitochondria need multiple B-vitamins, sulfur, antioxidants, coenzyme Q10, omega-3 essential fatty oils, and iodine to thrive and power our bodies.

Terry Wahls, M.D. is a living testament to mitochondria's critical role in our bodies. In a 2011 TedX Talk,[8] she described herself as the "canary in the coal mine." She was diagnosed with Multiple Sclerosis, and initially took the pharmaceutical route to combat her disease, only to watch her health deteriorate. She researched what was chemically happening to her brain and body and learned more about feeding her mitochondria. After 9 months, she successfully overcame her condition through proper nutrition and proved that ailments can be avoided if one is properly nourished.

Dr. Wahls determined that 9 cups of produce daily was sufficient to properly nourish our mitochondria. She accomplished this by consuming three cups of greens, (kale, chard, spinach, etc.) three cups of sulfur-rich veggies, (broccoli, asparagus, onions, etc.) and three cups of colorful produce (beets, carrots, berries, etc.) You may think it impossible to eat so much produce daily but it's easier than you think. One of the smartest health investments you can make is purchasing a high quality blender. Once

---

M.D. YouTube, 2010. Film. https://www.youtube.com/watch?v=5VWi6dXCT7I

[8] *Minding Your Mitochondria: Dr. Terry Wahls at TEDx Iowa City.* Dir. TedX Talk. Perf. Terry Wahls, M.D.. YouTube, 2011. Film. https://www.youtube.com/watch?v=KLjgBLwH3Wc

you get past sticker-shock, you begin to wonder how you ever lived without it. You can make green smoothies, fresh hummus and salsas, soup stocks, full meals, even grind flours from whole grains. Additional servings of produce becomes a non-issue.

Dr. Wahls also added high quality proteins to her diet, including grass-fed foods. These livestock are fed only mother's milk and allowed to graze freely on pasture grasses or consume greens and hay. Compared to conventionally produced meats and dairy, these leaner foods contain more healthy fats and have higher concentrations of vitamins, nutrients, and antioxidants, leaving you satiated. If your grocer doesn't offer grass-fed, a great resource for finding local producers and learning about food labels and farming practices is www.eatwild.com. In addition, www.localharvest.org offers an extensive state-categorized list of organic producers, farmer's markets and co-ops.

Admittedly, these foods are costlier but don't let that deter you. It's far less expensive than missed work, doctor bills, pharmaceuticals, surgeries and disease. By including more fresh produce, you've already upped your nutrient intake. You can then begin replacing the foods listed below with organic versions. These items are collectively known as the "dirty dozen" because they contain the highest pesticide levels of all produce.

Apples	Strawberries	Grapes	Celery
Peaches	Spinach	Bell Peppers	Cucumbers
Cherry Tomatoes	Potatoes	Nectarines (imported)	Snap Peas (imported)

The intestinal track is also one of our most vital and at times overlooked organs. An Albert-Ludwigs-Universität Freiburg research study ascertained our gut flora is essential to forming our immunity and that imbalances there lead to food allergies and/or chronic inflammatory intestinal diseases[9]. The simplest way to monitor food sensitivities is using a food diary. Noting how you feel after meals provides insight to intolerances. Did you experience indigestion? Often eating smaller, more frequent meals can solve this problem. Are you noticing a protein sensitivity, such as to casein and/or gluten? There are soy and coconut dairy options as well as gluten-free foods to help you avoid these proteins. Just remember that these foods sometimes have fillers such as refined white rice, sugar, and salt. Read your labels.

By reaping the benefit of better nutrition, I've effortlessly lost 20 pounds. My hips rarely trouble me and I sleep soundly. I'm working out again. I'm more energetic and have more mental clarity. My friends ask me what I've done to my skin and my hairdresser mentioned my hair had grown significantly since my last visit. And while a slight pinkness remains in my cheeks, I remind myself that this is a process. Although I haven't reached my ultimate goal, I'm thankful I'm not where I used to be.

While eating this way won't cure all illness, it has impacted my health in ways I couldn't have previously imagined. I hope my story inspires you to give yourself the gift of a healthy eating lifestyle. We don't realize how badly we've been feeling until we feel good. Once you regain your health, you'll never want to lose it again. Remember even simple changes, duplicated over time, create cumulative results. Invest in your health and it will be yours for life.

To contact Terry:

Here at *Your Health 4 Life*, we are dedicated to enriching your personal understanding of your body and helping you to achieve the healthiest lifestyle you possibly can. Over the years we've accumulated a plethora of knowledge regarding inflammation and natural healing. We also proudly offer preventative and reparative health care products and embrace what is considered by many to be the imminent medicine realm of bioelectrical/frequency devices. These devices measure and analyze

---

[9] Albert-Ludwigs-Universität Freiburg. "Natural Intestinal Flora Strengthen Immune System." ScienceDaily, 2 July 2012. www.sciencedaily.com/releases/2012/07/120702152940.htm

bioelectrical phenomena in the body and are designed to send corrective frequencies, perform bio-monitoring functions, and detect nutritional deficiencies. For more information about our products and services, or to learn more about fighting inflammation, reducing pain, and improving your overall health, visit us at http://yourhealth4life.leadpages.net/thechange

DR. JON C. HAASS

Dr. Haass works with clients across the nation seeking to transform their leadership in personal life and at work. Born and raised in Casper, Wyoming under clear starry skies, he gained an appreciation for nature and the scientific and mathematical methods of understanding life. Learning and teaching has remained a passion since receiving a PhD at MIT where he stayed on as CLE Moore Instructor while co-founding his first company. He has held executive and management roles in Sun Microsystems, OpenTV and Sendmail. Leadership and mentoring others to fully express their talents and purpose continues to be a source of joy. Trained in the Coaching and Leadership programs with Coach Training Institute; Dr. Haass has added the co-active and integral models to his work in the last decade with executives and teams. He recently accepted a position as Professor and Director of a new program in Cyber Intelligence and Security within The College of Security and Intelligence at Embry-Riddle University in Prescott, Arizona.

THE CHANGE IN LEADERSHIP

By Dr. Jon C. Haass

"We must learn to work with life in all its dimensions, seen and unseen." - Margaret Wheatley, from *Leadership and the New Science*

The last twenty five years have witnessed a shift toward new technologies that could beforehand only be called stranger than fiction. Consider just a few examples among the hundreds of developments we are experiencing. Knowledge surpassing any written encyclopedia is constantly being updated with authors and editors distributed around the globe – Wikipedia. Amazon, the 7 by 24 online one stop shopping center, is even considering using unmanned aerial vehicles to deliver packages. This innovation and change - thanks to internet technology and the commoditizing of computing and communication - has far reaching consequences. Leaders and leadership practices are impacted by the obvious as well as the hidden ramifications of the change in our work, play, conversation and travel.

Nowhere is this as clear as in the exchange and creation of information. Knowledge is and always has been power. Optimal intelligence is critical for leadership decisions, and the pressure to respond has intensified as the pace of news and the speed that news travels have both dramatically increased. We have come to accept that there is no such thing as complete information; and it is the art and science of today's leader to optimize, synthesize and decide based on the best available, but usually incomplete understanding. Mistakes are inevitable and must be expected; resiliency and recovery being key aspects of the new leader.

This chapter focuses on the change in leadership of self, of others, in collaboration and in the world. The evolutionary language of spiral dynamics and integral theory provides a framework to create a single cloth from these different threads.

Leadership and the Self

> "Self-deception obscures the truth about ourselves, corrupts our view of others and our circumstances, and inhibits our ability to make wise and helpful decisions" - Arbinger Institute, from *Leadership and Self Deception*

A clear, practical sense of one's life direction is necessary to reach great goals in such an emerging landscape. But even more is needed to create excellent outcomes in today's complex workplace settings – uncommon skills that often cannot be found in conventional training and upbringing. It is a courageous conversation, as poet David Whyte refers to it, that we must engage with, one that is sometimes off limits or threatening but precisely where the inquiry must begin.

Surrounded by data, daily routines, and fires to put out, the cornerstone to these emerging leadership traits is an intimate understanding of our own interior landscape. To know thyself is a wonderful maxim, yet to access our deeper powers of insight and will often requires a special journey that combines our inner imagination, wit and skill. Today, with the ground around moving at the speed of information, no wonder people are saying "I can't keep up." I don't have time to listen to who or what I am. The seduction of instant global communication at every hour pulls constantly away from our own sacred ground of self. The challenge is to trust that within the chaos, a new order is emerging. Resisting the change is like swimming against the undertow, ultimately the struggle overwhelms even the strongest.

The frontier has already arrived, the conversation is already underway and each of us must dare to jump onboard. Never fear that we must go somewhere to catch up with the change, the world is gladly bringing it daily to our doorstep. The new leader accepts him or her as a continuously changing and growing part of this global system, participating in and vulnerable to its ebb and flow. Any notion of doing it perfectly is far too rigid and brittle and inevitably results in breakage. The force of the forward moving storm is too great and is sweeping us all to a new world. And there will be destruction along the way. Like any natural system, parts must be shed; old patterns must dissolve to make room for the new. Our own favorite ways may have to also be released and retooled. A leader that demands a steady as she goes approach will be disillusioned and may go back to old ways of holding power, warrior force (red) or my way or highway thinking (blue). We see through the lens of spiral dynamics how the simple survival responses by themselves cannot keep us safe or secure. We are not battling tigers any longer and a new intuition must overcome fight and flight.

As a leader today, traversing unprecedented change at an increased pace, learning to embrace parts of our self beyond ideas and rational mechanics is essential. We are, in fact, finding this new leader within - through both skillful best practices and faith. Outside-the-box vocabulary becomes more commonplace in describing this new edge. The yellow, turquoise, and coral "memes" of the global era become more central. These concepts from spiral dynamics can be found in far greater detail in the work of Don Beck and Ken Wilbur, here summarized in a table of evolving leadership attributes:

First tier – Local thinking – Limited viewpoint – Quarterly						Second tier – Global thinking		
Beige	Purple	Red	Blue	Orange	Green	Yellow	Turquoise	Coral
Survival	Tribal	Warrior	Crusade	Inventor	Connector	Systemic	Holistic	Imaginative

The change from first tier survivalist thinking to second tier global awareness is already here; it is just not practiced by many and mastered by even fewer. The very definition of the emerging tier of leadership is the ability to integrate all the previous modes of being and acting while synthesizing and responding upon a far larger stage.

Critical leadership conversation of the self relies on accepting the grace of the moment; the wisdom to see false ideas that hold our own protective masks firmly in place. But hiding behind the mask cannot provide what was hoped, an invincibility, a hoped for protection from being discovered. Most people live with invisible beliefs that hold them back from operating at their full potential. Too much energy is being spent on maintaining their worldview and then accepting the impact on their health and relationships. These limiting beliefs prevent honestly knowing who you really are.

You may be one of the lucky ones to have already discovered some of these old stories like "I have to work hard to be successful," "If I let down my guard, people will take advantage of me," and the list goes on. But maybe you still get triggered when people appear unhappy with you, perhaps you become uncomfortable when people express strong emotions, perhaps you respond with your own power plays of anger, voice raising (warrior – red), there are innumerable examples that provide the clue that you are resisting and defending the world around you.

We come into life with the self-view of acceptance and powerful alignment, feeling when things are not in our self-interest. However, quickly we fall into the dream taught by family, parents, teachers that in subtle or even harsh ways communicate that we are not good enough unless we are performing and meeting the standards set by others. Truth is - You are already capable to be you.

To be an effective agent of organizational and cultural change, the mastery of one's own *effectual* sense of self is the first stepping stone to sharing leadership with others. The next is the focus and commitment to interact with others in increasingly constructive manner to generate meaningful, if not exceptional team outcomes.

Leadership and Other

> "Trust men and they will be true to you: treat them greatly and they will show themselves great." - Ralph Waldo Emerson

In the global environment we learn from every level, subatomic to the cellular to interpersonal, that we are constantly engaged in relationship. Forever moving in and out of relationship with something or someone, and with the skills learned in relating to self in a true and honest way, more of our energy and clear presence is available to meet the events that are made up by these local and global relationships.

Looking again through the lens of spiral dynamics, we see the same stages (survival to holistic action) appearing in leadership with others as they play out in our own internal development.

Survival level is recognizing that other people are at their own stage of grappling with their self-mastery and leadership. Their response to you being more a reflection of their own internal working than a true interaction with what you are saying or doing. Until we have cleaned up sufficiently our own lens of view, relationships quickly become extremely messy - as prejudice, beliefs, poor listening filters and reactive actions escalate without either party understanding what just happened.

If you have significant intimate relationships with spouse, children or close friends, you have witnessed this first hand. Why did they get so upset when I just came home and said... or did some simple thing that turned into world war next.

These actions are difficult with just one person. To navigate with a team or entire organization filled with people who are shifting in and out of all different stages from survival to enlightened global thinker demands higher level capabilities. Organizations today seek the emerging holistic emotional skill sets and acknowledge imaginative (turquoise) interpersonal abilities as requirement for next generation leaders. Indeed the change demands leaders be competent with relations of every type that may shift from collective (green) to stubborn (blue) within minutes. The facility to remain fully engaged with others while survival meme struggles are being played out requires a detached observer awareness and systemic understanding (yellow).

Shared Leadership

> "Accept the fact that we have to treat almost anybody as a volunteer...." - Peter Drucker

Shared leadership is an approach just now coming into its own. Spiral dynamics says the leading edge of humanity is moving beyond the green meme into the yellow and turquoise. This is where you are likely to be spending more of your time, and others strive to be. It is global; it sees the one-ness of people while valuing individual talents and gifts. Shared leadership moves beyond majority rule and the hierarchy that is rapidly flattening. It is discovering that each person must choose to fully participate in order to achieve their individual greatness. In the end, no one can be forced to be creative or visionary.

To be a leader in the world today, one must move out from behind the older image of leadership. One is asked to let go of the mask that "demands" respect (blue) due to some position or implied authority. As more of the world recognizes the power of choice, new ways of operating open up. Silent bystanders have a voice with Tweets, posts, email and YouTube reporting. The natural urge to contribute, to be recognized, to creatively offer your own position as part of the conversation stirs inside every person and demands more of the true leader.

Shared leadership is supporting collaboration and valuing the work of each member of organization or team. Now, we can find the leaders where they already exist. In the changing world, leaders appear. They stand up and imaginatively act according to their conviction and passion, usually not asking for permission (coral).

In a growing number of organizations and global settings we are seeing the emergence of shared leadership. Today's health care leaders are confronted with unprecedented change. Some large health organizations have formally embraced shared leadership. Administration, doctors, nurses, staff and patients come together with a common goal of improved service, reduced cost and better working conditions. If enhanced health is the goal and that is measured by the outcome of patients; it is natural to include the entire community leadership in its achievement.

In more informal settings, the wisdom of including all perspectives can guide decisions in a distributed manner insuring that light is shed from all directions. This allows action to take place where and when it is needed without the delay of standard operating procedures or normal chain of command. This has been seen in the local response to tragedies where first responders lead from the holistic and imaginative view; there is work to be done and I am here and able. The genius of a shared leader is to harness that far-flung talent by providing the vision and rallying the resources to create effective outcomes. It is the ultimate form of calling greatness forward from life's volunteers.

Leadership and the Changing World

> "Almost always, the creative dedicated minority has made the world better" - Martin Luther King Jr.

Today's information age leader must not only master honest and authentic group communications, she must also craft and extend conversations on a global scale. Living in integrity, with sustainability, new leaders recognize the everyday actions that add up to differences unknown or unrecognized at the time. Although this globally aware action may seem mundane, the ripple as a leader is magnified by those touched personally and through that extended network.

This time of change is a time of awakening and transformation on many scales. The number and variety of teachers offering interpretations and tools for individuals and organizations to grow is unprecedented. This has emerged and evolved at such speed largely thanks to the information revolution. Print on demand, webinars, tele-seminars, blogs, and inexpensive communication can reach large audiences everywhere. Author and sociologist Paul Ray in the 1999 book *Cultural Creative* estimated 60 million people around the globe were seeking personal and leadership growth. This group represents the vanguard of a new more human-centric era where a leader can choose to inspire from anywhere and reach global audiences.

This interconnected and interdependent world can seem like an overwhelming complexity of contradictory forces. Freedoms clashing against national security interests, transparency of information and closely guarded intellectual property point to insurmountable duality. If we take a cue from natural forces like the weather, the seasonal and daily extremes can be seen on a scale far larger than any single event or generation.

Consider what we see today with strong nationalistic and fundamentalist movements wrestling for dominance. While portions of the world are experimenting with new concepts characterized in the spiral dynamic language as inclusive (green), entrepreneurial (orange), or even globally aware (yellow and turquoise), nearly a billion people still struggle with daily survival (beige) and lack available clean water. It is no wonder then that another larger population remains locked in step with single focus belief systems (blue) that are intolerant of those that are different.

The availability of communication and information about the human face of people across the globe has been shown to help connect at a personal level. A level where there is the compassion to realize that each person ultimately cares about self, family and loved ones. When these basics are threatened, the warrior arises in anger and outrage (red), and if a villain can be identified this energy can be rallied as we see in uprisings and terrorism throughout the world.

It is possible to connect at that personal level. The population is capable of nearly instant communication. News becomes available not only from large media organizations and governments but also from individual bloggers, tweets and cellular connections. The 2014 coverage of a Malaysia Air commercial airline downed over disputed territory with the flurry of information and disinformation from numerous sources is only an early indication of the power of "volunteer reporters" armed with a smart phone now capable of posting news clips. These in turn picked up and amplified by media outlets.

And it is almost impossible to shut down this kind of information since there is no single company or station that can be forced under injunction to cease. The information genie is released and global leadership will have to learn to use these new and powerful social media tools.

Again we see a trend from few voices, to many voices, to the future where everyone has a voice. Of course not everyone will have the amplifying power of a head of state, a pope, a soccer star or famous actress. Nevertheless, out of all of the cacophony of internet enabled media, an order arises and it is like weather in constant change. And within that a vast storehouse of information is created from which new and meaningful ideas will arise. New leaders emerge as well.

A young woman brings solar technology to provide a cheaper way to create distilled water from even the worst water sources. The invention uses easily manufactured components to generate power, the liter of clean water per day a beneficial side effect. The concept is funded through an internet crowd sourcing site. This is the face of new global leadership in action. It was said it can't be done. A leader hears that as a challenge and not believing the limitation says, "I may not solve the whole world's problem, but I can solve a worldwide problem for some of the people that suffer from it." And the ripple of change begins.

As they thrive, these inspired global leaders operate from an imaginative, flexible values-based vision - allowing those around them, and following them, to shine as well.

> "The truth is that most of life will unfold in accordance with forces far outside your control, regardless of what your mind says" - Michael A. Singer, *The Untethered Soul: The Journey Beyond Yourself*

What we do get to control, through our choices moment to moment, is what we make that unfolding mean. Is it a "yes" to the possible, or a negative bias, "can't do it." Your world around and leadership experience will fully participate in the change with that simple but not easy choice.

For more information on Dr. Jon Haass work:

Contact: MyCoach@JonHaass.com Website: JonHaass.com

CARMEN TAYLOR

Women Success Mentor Carmen Taylor guides successful women in business and emerging business experts to live a Blissfully Wealthy life through helping them to get what they want and loving every bit of it. Weather her mentees seek to attract clients, break through their income ceiling or create wealth and success; they learn to manifest those results by acting on Carmen's proven advice to live in abundance and blissful wealth. Best of all, they create the wealth and success they desire and fill their lives with blissfulness that translate into happiness in all areas of their lives. Carmen doesn't just dole out this advice. She walks her own talk. Born in Panama City, Panama; Carmen has been both poor and wealthy, but to her surprised she was miserable at both ends. Realizing that graduating from Engineering school, obtaining an MBA from an Ivy League School, and earning a top 1% income wasn't enough, she had to discover the way to conquer depression and love her wealth and her life. Today, Carmen lives Blissfully Wealthy as a wife, mother and woman in business herself, hosting The Carmen Taylor Show: Soulful Success Secrets for Women in Business and as the Official SelfGrowth.com Guide to Success Coaching.

LIVING BLISSFULLY WEALTHY

Getting What You Want and Loving Every Bit of It

By Carmen Taylor

"Blissfully Wealthy" is a term that I coined after years of feeling completely miserable and tired of pretending that I was happy with all the things that I had.

In the eyes of the world, I had it all, but no one really knew how unhappy and depressed I felt every day of my life.

It's like I always knew that I was meant to do and be more, but I wasn't quite sure what that was. In fact, I spent many years of my life just wishing for the next day to come, just hoping that it would be better than the last one. To my surprise, the days never got better. In fact, they kept getting lonelier and sadder.

It wasn't like I didn't try to find something to fill that void. In fact, I did more than the average person, just trying to find some significance in the world.

I was born in Panama City, Panama, to a lower-middle-class family, and I never had much of anything. I was lucky to attend private schools, as I had scholarships throughout school and college, and I graduated with honors at the age of 22 with a double engineering degree.

Pursuing my desire to be more than a typical Latin-American working-class woman, after landing a very good job at the local brewery, I decided to get an MBA from the best graduate school on the planet. Against all odds, I was admitted to and graduated from a regional business school founded by Harvard Business School.

The story of how I was able to earn the funds to go to graduate school is interesting and inspiring, and demonstrates my determination to prove that I wanted more.

As a result of my accomplishments, I was offered three positions with Fortune 500 companies in the United States. At the age of 24, I moved to Silicon Valley, California after accepting one of these jobs.

You might say that life was pretty good for me. After all, I was under 25 years old, making $75,000 per year, and living the life in San Francisco. Yet I was not happy.

I used to be fascinated by people who were happy despite their circumstances. In particular, I remember one such person whom, to keep her privacy, I'm going to call Carrie. She was dating my ex-husband's roommate. That girl always had a smile on her face.

I found it annoying that although her boyfriend Dave treated her like a second-class citizen, Carrie was so happy and grateful to be with him.

At the time, because I didn't know how someone could be that happy, I thought that she was either faking it or really naive.

Years passed, and I married my ex-husband. We had it all on the outside: a nice house, nice cars, lots of travel, country club parties in the Bay Area, etc. However, the reality is that I had a huge, empty space inside me. I was completely miserable.

It was not my ex's fault. He is a good man, and today we have a very good relationship, not only as co-parents to our kids, but also as friends.

The truth is that he didn't stand a chance of making me happy because no one can make another person happy. Happiness comes from within.

After the birth of my son Stefan, something clicked inside me. I decided that it was time to wake up and find out what happiness really was. After all, if there was something that I wanted to show and teach this little guy, it was that.

After a lot of soul searching, I realized that real happiness, the one that I call Blissfulness today, was something that I needed to create from the inside out.

It finally clicked for me that all the riches, all the investments, all the wealth, nice cars, mansions, vacation homes, expensive clothes - none of those things would fill the void that I had inside.

Around that time, I also realized that even though my son had made me feel love for the first time in my life, not even he could make me happy.

Moreover, it was not my son's job to fulfill my needs and I wasn't about to task him with an impossible mission like that so early in his life.

Aware of my desires and challenges, I decided to find happiness. I started searching for real, honest answers to my unknown and burning questions.

I listened to many motivational teachers, among them Abraham-Hicks. One of the first things that stuck in my head was their quote: "Your Job is not to figure out how. Your Job is to get clear on what you want."

That's when I realized that I couldn't get "happy" if I didn't know what happiness meant for me. As with success, happiness is a relative state of emotions defined by each individual, and is never the same for two people.

Like I mentioned earlier, Carrie was happy with her life, though I thought it was rather pathetic. That meant only that her definition of happiness and my definition of happiness were totally different, both back then and I'm sure to this day.

I had embarked on my journey, and the first obstacle that I had to overcome was to develop my own definition of happiness.

What is Living Blissfully Wealthy?

My pattern in life has always been to exceed even my own expectations.

I love to go the extra mile every time. I thrive by exceeding goals and previous performances. That is just who I am.

As you can imagine, for me, defining happiness wasn't going to be any different.

After all, at that point I'd been miserable for 31 years. I figured, instead of being happy, what if I became something more so that I could account for the lost time.

I thought and thought for days and nights - while I was breastfeeding Stefan, while I was in the shower, while I was driving - all the free time that I had.

I thought and I thought and I thought some more about what it was that I wanted. What would make me happier than happy?

Finally, I came to love a particular idea. I wanted Extreme Happiness, Ecstasy, and Spiritual Joy, but I also wanted to love and feel loved. I wanted to feel an abundance of material and divine gifts. I wanted to be Blissfully Wealthy.

I understood that to embark on Blissfully Wealthy Living, I had to totally eradicate from my life depression, misery, sadness, sorrow, and all feelings of unhappiness, including feelings of scarcity and feelings that I did not have enough.

I had been poor growing up, and I didn't want to live paycheck to paycheck ever again.

I was lonely growing up and I was lonely in my marriage, and I never, ever wanted to feel lonely again, even if I was alone.

Now that I was cruising along with the Law of Attraction principles, I wanted to believe with every cell of my body that the Universe would always provide abundance and opportunities for me, and that all I needed to do was be open to them.

Why is it Important to Live Blissfully Wealthy?

Did you know that the number of wealthy people is growing in the United States every year? And at a faster rate than ever before?

Did you also know that at the same time, the percentage of people with depression is increasing at a rate of 15 percent per year?

Even worse, the National Institute of Mental Health claims that a strong correlation exists between wealth and depression, especially in women.

With this kind of evidence, now more than ever, it's important to be a little selfish and take care of our own needs first.

Untreated depression can be a serious problem. It increases the incidence of risk behaviors, such as drug or alcohol addiction. It can also ruin relationships, cause problems at work, and make it difficult to overcome serious illnesses.

Depression affects the way a person eats and sleeps. It affects the way a person feels about himself or herself and those around him or her. It even affects a person's thoughts and destiny.

It's like a Catch-22 really, because without wealth, a person is likely to have some type of depression, especially when financial problems arise.

However, with wealth, a person might experience the same thing unless he or she figures out a way to be both Wealthy and Happy. That's exactly what I'm talking about here: Living Blissfully Wealthy.

There is another angle that I see often with my clients. They work so hard to get the wealth to which they aspire, and to provide a better life for their families, that they often feel burned out, overworked, and overwhelmed… sometimes to the point that they want to throw in the towel. This is especially true for business owners.

This happens because when a person spends his or her life working hard to make money, he or she assumes that happiness will follow. However, while earning the money that is supposed to make him or her happy, the person misses great moments, memories, and precious times with his or her family. This makes the person unhappy because he or she has missed the most important parts of his or her life while achieving something irrelevant. After all, money is just a tool to reach one's ultimate goal: to Be Happy. Isn't that what everyone wants?

As a success coach, I've seen it time after time: all the goals and all the dreams that my clients want to accomplish in their lives and in their businesses ultimately create happiness in their lives.

How Does One Become Blissfully Wealthy?

Today I'm Living Blissfully Wealthy. I'm happily married to the love of my life; I have two amazing kids (and one on the way); and I have a very fulfilling business. I have happiness, bliss, and wealth. I'm living proof that you, too, can have it all.

However, when I decided to start this journey, I made some hefty mistakes. The purpose of my chapter in this book is to help you avoid making most, if not all, of the mistakes that I made.

You see, about three years passed between the time that I first clarified what Blissfully Wealthy meant for me and the day that I could actually and honestly say out loud that I was living Blissfully Wealthy.

The reason that the process took so long was that I did not listen to my intuition. In fact, I constantly argued with it, even though I knew that I needed to make some serious decisions in my life. I was still caught up in the idea of living my life to please others.

I grew up trying to find my significance through my mother, trying to do anything in my power to please her, just to fail over and over again. That's why when I realized that I'd made a mistake and that I needed to divorce my ex-husband, it took me about three years, many tears, and countless sad days to convince myself that I would never be happy if I was going to keep pleasing the world.

It wasn't a matter of being selfish and hurting others. "What if I wait until the kids go to college? That's just another 15 years." This thought kept crossing my mind and even found its way into a conversation that I had with my ex. Thankfully sanity came to me and I recognized that I could give my kids so much more by being authentically happy instead of pretending to be happy. At the end of the day, the only one getting fooled was me.

Finally, I took a leap of faith and grabbed control of my life, Emotionally, Spiritually, and Financially.

It was at that moment that my real journey toward Living Blissfully Wealthy began.

As you embark on your own journey toward becoming Blissfully Wealthy, the first thing you must understand is what makes you happy.

There are six areas that every human must fulfill in his or her life. The magic is finding out, for you, which area is most important.

The six areas are:

1. Security
2. Adventure
3. Love

4. Meaning

5. Influence

6. Heritage

For me, meaningfulness is important. I need to live my purpose. It wasn't until I accepted this fact that my whole universe experienced a constant "upward-spiral" effect.

After you have discovered what makes you happy, you can start the process of Living Blissfully Wealthy Ever After.

I have an entire program that can guide you through the process in 10 weeks. This is a step-by-step, proven guide that will take you by the hand and show you how to Become Blissfully Wealthy. Keep reading and I'll give you an overview of the same steps that have transformed my clients' lives and my own.

Note that for some people, knowing the steps is enough to create change, while others need a little more handholding. That's why I have in my website three levels of support, tailored for every budget and every need.

This is just the beginning of an exciting journey for you, and I'm so thrilled and excited to be right here to support you in the process.

Living Blissfully Wealthy is the most amazing feeling anyone can experience. Trust me—once you experience it for yourself, you are going to want to share it with the world.

My proven process consists of seven steps that, when done in the right order and with consistency, are guaranteed to catapult your life into a permanent state of Bliss and Wealth.

The real secret for succeeding with this process is to eradicate old, limiting habits and to replace them with new, empowering actions, thoughts, and feelings that together will exponentially support your desire to have it all.

1. Wealth Attunement and Conditioning

2. Modern Application of the Universal Laws

3. Galvanizing your Greatness and Gifts

4. Leveraging your Time and Money

5. Implementing Successful Business Strategies

6. Vibrational Level Awareness and Correction

7. Compounding Wealth Growth

I teach my clients to become Blissfully Wealthy by incrementally and progressively integrating each of these steps into their lives.

Some of these steps can be taught and implemented right away, while others must be added using a dropper-like technique.

In addition to the seven steps that I mention above, for faster and more permanent results, I recommend daily meditations, starting at lengths of at least three minutes per day, then undertaking progressively longer sessions. For ultimate results, you should maintain a goal of at least eight minutes a day. The more you meditate, the better the results you will get.

Also, fully and constantly clarifying your own definition of happiness is key. That said, you are welcome to use my definition of Living Blissfully Wealthy as I shared it with you previously: "Extreme Happiness, Ecstasy, and Abundance of Love and Divine Gifts."

Finally, you must dramatically replace old limiting habits with new empowering ones. Beliefs can be tricky to break. Because you created your current belief system as a self-defense mechanism, you might find that at times, your beliefs are misleading.

Once you recognize this, you will realize that you can create new neurological paths in your brain. These paths will replace your old, disempowering beliefs with a new set of supercharged, empowering ones that won't allow anything in your mind but the pure inspiration that you need to create the Blissfully Wealthy Life that you want.

One way to accomplish this is by replacing your Automatic Negative Thoughts with Automatic Positive Thoughts, using the right types of meditations and brain wave sounds, and having support from someone who cares about your success and who calls you out when you are focusing on perfection instead of progress. This is a guaranteed recipe for success.

This is a journey, and as such, takes time. My journey took three years, but yours doesn't have to take that long.

Remember that, as with any new process, changes must occur and that getting used to these changes takes time.

Some people are great at adapting to new situations, while others do best when they have support systems that give them encouragement, accountability, mentorship, and community.

Whatever approach works for you, stick to it.

You, too, deserve to Live Blissfully Wealthy!

I know you can do it.

Carmen Taylor, Women Success Coach and C.E.O. (Creator of Extraordinary Opportunities) at Carmen Taylor, LLC is dedicated to help women in business create success and live a Blissfully Wealthy Life.

You can learn more about Carmen at:

www.Carmen-Taylor.com

www.BlissfullyWealthyMastermind.com

The Change

DEBORAH ANDERSON

Deborah Anderson, Certified Life Coach and student of The Law of Attraction, has studied, interpreted and presented what makes people successful and happy. She knows what motivates them, what drives them, and what inspires them to make changes in their lives. In her coaching practice, Deborah brings forth these critical insight and success strategies helping countless people live a more fulfilling life.

Her ability to dig right in and solve problems is her forte. Deborah is known for helping her students achieve happier, more focused, more effective lives by understanding how to increase emotional energy, make critical decisions, and overcome limiting beliefs that keep people from living the life they want and deserve.

MY JOURNEY TO COMPASSION

By Deborah Anderson

Early on in life I learned that it is best to be quiet, not to say anything, to stay in the background, and then I will be safe. My haven was playing outside either by myself or with my brother and sister on our 130 acre dairy farm, where we were allowed to wander about and experience all sorts of outside adventures playing in the creek, climbing trees, making huts. This is where I learned to love nature. I am so grateful that we were able to do this, and were not over-supervised and worried over. My father loved trees, and there were many shelter belts planted on the farm that were wonderful adventure sites to explore.

School was a very uncomfortable experience. I didn't have friends until the last year or two of primary school, and then I was off to secondary school without my friends as they went to other schools. I felt disconnected at secondary school and I didn't know who I was any more. I discovered boys, drugs and alcohol – wonderful tools for covering up my disconnectedness and feeling of being lost. My first relationship with a boyfriend didn't last very long, as I was being good and staying quietly in the background, which doesn't work well in relationships. After that I moved to Australia, not only lost but now lost and lonely. Interestingly, employment and money were never an issue; my childhood on the farm had given me a great work ethic, and I have always enjoyed being of assistance.

As time went by, I felt ready to be a mother, and within a year my son Sean was on the way. I had so much love for him. He opened my heart and taught me to love. A very friendly, outgoing and loving child, he welcomed everyone enthusiastically. He loved experiencing new things and everything had to be investigated and explored.

Just before his second birthday, I decided it was time to move back to New Zealand. My family were not the same as the people he was accustomed to having around him. They were accepting but not demonstrative, and I felt sad for him and the sense of loss he felt.

One lovely sunny spring day, I decided it was too nice a day to go about our normal routine, and instead we went to the beach for the day. We saw a man walking alone in the distance, and in his usual outgoing way Sean ran up to him – "Hullo man!" And that is how I met my husband… We are still married 29 years later, and have two lovely daughters.

For Sean, growing up and being in the education system of the 1980's with undiagnosed ADHD was not a good experience. ADHD was not recognized then, so he was treated as being naughty and was sometimes smacked; as a result of which he became quiet and withdrawn and less trusting of people. He enjoyed university and did very well there. He eventually moved to Australia for work, which went well for a time, however he didn't seem able to make friends, and found it difficult to settle in there - so much so that he became unwell. I went to stay with him while he was in hospital and recovering – diagnosis Psychosis. Three months after he recovered, he resigned from his job and returned to New Zealand. He was not very happy living at home, and there was no employment available in the field that he had trained in for about a year, when an opportunity came up in Christchurch. He moved there, though he was reluctant to leave this area and his friends. It was a good job and he did very well at it, but the feelings of isolation persisted.

Then came a phone call from his employer. He had taken some days leave and hadn't returned to work. Is he with us? No. The knock on our door came at 3am, the police had found him. The pain, the physical gut wrenching pain… I felt like I had run into a brick wall at 100kph. The weather became grey, cloudy and raining too, to match how I was feeling.

Not knowing how to deal with the pain and grief of the loss of a child, not knowing what to do, how to handle it, trying to push it down and not feel it. It was too big. I reached rock bottom a month later, on my birthday, coming home after work to find the house in complete disarray – burglars having gone through everything.

The worst thing was the theft of his mobile phone (along with other things), which was part of a shrine I had created in honor of his memory. Reaching out for help, I contacted Jeanette Wilson, the psychic medium who helped me "just notice how you are feeling, don't try and change it in any way, just notice…" What a difference those words made to me. I was now more able to observe the pain and not be so consumed by it. This was the first step in healing and I was determined to be OK – "The phoenix shall rise from the ashes". I knew there was a long way to go, but I was now on the way. Every time I felt bad I would send him love; I didn't want him to be suffering any more, which helped me to feel better as well. It was a change of focus.

I planted 30 walnut trees in memory of him, surrounding each one with his ashes. I am with him when I am with the trees.

I was out there one day with the trees, thinking it would be my retirement project and I could live happily and peacefully there, growing and selling walnuts and hazelnuts, when it came to me that "No, you're not finished yet, you can enjoy the trees, but you have come here for more than that."

"Your work is to discover your work, and then with all your heart to give yourself to it" – Gautama Buddha.

I began attending things, a weekly Practical Philosophy group, psychic development workshops, Vipassana meditation courses, and I learned Reiki and auric magnetic healing.

I attended a wonderfully healing supportive Astrology weekend workshop with Deirdre Wilton, and from that learned that my work to fulfill my life purpose appeared to be healing through communication. My initial reaction to this was "Communication! I can't talk to people - no." I felt terrified! But if that is what I am here to do, then so be it, and so I began my search for how I could do this.

I thought about studying counseling, but when I looked at the content of the course, it didn't feel right for me at all. I almost signed up for a two year massage course but then I discovered Life Coaching, and the more I looked at it, the more I knew it was right for me.

I was accepted into the Life Coach Associates coaching course, and I was really enjoying it. The first three modules were about our own journey; with the idea that you can't take anyone where you haven't been yourself. Then it was time to learn about Coaching Skills, and by the end of the first day I felt so much fear. I felt sick, unable to drive home, unable to do anything. I asked for a coaching session with one of the facilitators of the course and the session was so liberating. I was able to find where the fear (of speaking, of people) was in my body. I was able to breathe through it and come out the other side, where I was then able to release it.

This was the beginning of a huge change. My confidence was increasing. I was now able to see myself as a Life Coach. This experience gave me absolute confidence in the Life Coaching process. It works. My confidence continues to increase, and with it, my eagerness to introduce other aspects into my practice. I have a real interest in the Law of Attraction, and the opportunity to be a Law of Attraction Coach through the Quantum Success Coaching Academy came up, which I am currently attending; and the journey is awesome.

Attending the weekly Practical Philosophy group helped me to start becoming more aware of my thoughts. We think about 60,000 thoughts each day; and if these thoughts are often negative and you continually beat yourself up for something you felt didn't go the way you wanted it to, it doesn't feel very good. This is how I used to be… so glad I am not any more.

I decided I wanted to change my thoughts to be more supporting and positive. I wore a bracelet that could be easily changed from one arm to the other, and set the intention to have only positive thoughts go through the gate of my mind – like drafting sheep. When I became aware of a negative thought, I changed the bracelet to the other arm (the sheep is drafted out of the yard).

This exercise did two things. It helped me to become more aware of my thoughts; and because I was more aware, it also helped me to change my thoughts to being more positive. I found that I would feel uncomfortable when I had a negative thought, and I began to realize that this was my own inner guidance at work. It didn't take long before changing my thoughts became a habit (which I still practice); and while the negative thoughts try to creep in quietly and unnoticed, I am much better equipped at letting them go.

However, self compassion is important in these moments - no beating yourself up if you observe a negative thought.

Vipassana, which means to see things as they really are, is one of India's most ancient techniques of meditation. It was taught in India more than 2,500 years ago. The technique of Vipassana Meditation is taught all over the world at ten day residential courses. The Vipassana Centre in New Zealand is set in a beautiful valley with a stream running through it and native bush on both sides. There is a track by the stream which mediators can walk along for exercise during the meal break times.

During the first three days, the meditation technique is focusing on the breathing, which helps to focus the attention. On the fourth day, the Vipassana technique is introduced. This is focusing on each part of the body in turn and noticing any sensations that may arise. One must observe equanimously anything that arises. This technique definitely helped me to become heaps more aware of what is happening in my body, and also my mind, at any given time.

During the first ten day Vipassana meditation course I attended, I had a lovely view of the bush from the door of my room. And as it was spring, the tree fern fronds were unfurling - to me, this signified new beginnings. Over the time of the course, I was able to change my view point from grieving and thinking about Sean not being with me any more, to being able to thank him for being with me for 26 years, for the times we had together, for opening my heart and teaching me how to love. It was so good to be able to come to terms with this, and not to carry the burden of grief around with me any more.

At the end of the next ten day Vipassana meditation course I attended, I was able to let go of all blame and negativity, and to thank my mother for giving me the freedom to play outside on the farm, to be able to learn and grow through my adventures, to see that it had been an ideal place to grow up, and that my childhood had been just exactly right for me. I realized and acknowledged that she had done the best that she could do. That forgiveness felt so good - it was so good to be able to let go of the blame and negative feelings around the lack of communication and feeling unloved.

The next Vipassana course I attended was about self compassion. I was feeling so homesick and unhappy, everything was dark and gloomy, and negative thoughts seemed to think themselves. I was heading into the downward spiral of depression. Once I was able to accept where I was and stopped fighting the depression and the negative thoughts, and instead focused on compassionate love and acceptance of where I was, I began to feel much better.

The Wikipedia meaning of compassion is: "The feeling of empathy for others. Compassion is the emotion that we feel in response to the suffering of others that motivates a desire to help. Feelings of kindness and forgiveness are also part of compassion." The Buddha says "Compassion is that which makes the heart of the good move at the pain of others. It crushes and destroys the pain of others; thus it is called compassion. It is called compassion because it shelters and embraces the distressed."

I was given two posters a few years ago, which I put on the wall in my meditation room, and I look at them each time I go in there. They provide much food for thought. The first one "You Must Be the Change you Wish to See in the World"- Mahatma Ghandi, gradually helped me to realize that you have the power to change anything you want to in the world by changing yourself. You can't wait for someone else to change, or to expect it to be done for you.

If you live life the way you want it to be – full of love, kindness, compassion and in harmony with yourself, others and the Earth - then it radiates out and affects those around you, and so affects those around them. You can't change anyone else, they have to do it for themselves; but by living the life you want they may also be inspired to be the change they wish to see in the world.

The second poster – "Your Beliefs Become Your Destiny"- Mahatma Ghandi, also provides much food for thought, and became a gradual realization that if I change what I believe, then I can change what happens in my life. This has been further validated for me since I started doing the Law of Attraction Coaching course which covers all the Universal Laws and how they work, and how they can be incorporated into coaching to help empower people to be able to live the lives they want.

The Law of Attraction states that what you focus on grows, so if you feel bad and focus on it, you get to feel worse. If you are focusing on judgmental, hateful thoughts about yourself not being good enough, or not being enough, they grow bigger and you can't see anything past this; even though there may be many positive things happening around you.

Once you are able to release all these judgmental and non-supporting thoughts, and instead fill yourself with love and kindness, it feels so much better. To accept yourself as you are, to have compassion for yourself, to know that you do your best with what you have – can you do any better than your best?

This is like "building your house on a rock." Once you are able to love yourself and accept yourself for who you are, you are not pushed about by everyone/everything any more. You stand strong in who you are and have so much more confidence, peace and happiness.

"Building your house on sand" is how I was as a teenager through to mid-adulthood, being affected by everyone around me, trying to please everyone, and ending up not pleasing anyone… least of all myself. I allowed myself to be shoved about all over the place, and it did not feel good at all. It felt dark and negative and I ended up blaming myself and everyone else for what was happening. I had endless thoughts about how bad I was and how I always mess up. I was never able to feel joy because I would always feel that something bad would happen if I felt too good. And because I believed that, it always happened.

If you can have compassion for yourself, you can then have compassion for others. You can then see that everyone is doing the best they can with the resources they have available at the time. If you know this, you can acknowledge that it is their journey, and not blame yourself or them for it. You can then take responsibility for your life and do what you can to create it how you want it. It is surprising what opportunities arise when you are open to them.

A willingness to start working on being compassionate is the first step. It is very easy to stand at the bottom of the mountain looking at the top and wondering how you are going to get there; and thinking it is too hard, so you don't make a start.

The second step is to make the intention to start – and once again to do your best. Thoughts are powerful beams of energy. Setting an intention is like throwing a rope over a post and using it as a support for your journey. You are never alone, there is always someone or something there to help you on the journey. It is interesting how people, books, opportunities and different information appear on your path to help.

See yourself getting there, know you can do it, and take small steps each day towards it. It may seem to be a long and winding journey, and sometimes you seem further away from the goal than you were the day before; but if you persevere you will get there.

Each day is one day closer to where you want to be – each minute, each second, you are in the process of getting there. The only thing stopping you from creating what you want is your beliefs. If you can change your beliefs, one thought at a time, then anything is possible. There is then nothing that you cannot be, do or have.

Be the Change you Wish to See....

For more information on Deborah's work:

Telephone: 0064 021 111 9399 New Zealand

Website: www.golifecoaching.net.nz

Facebook page: https://www.facebook.com/pages/Go-Life-Coaching-Ltd-Deborah-Anderson

JANICE ANGELA BURT

Janice Angela Burt is a court certified Spanish Interpreter, a voice-over artist, and an inspirational speaker. She is also currently training to become a certified yoga teacher. As a child, she lived in Mexico City for five years where her love for the Spanish language began. After returning to the United States, she settled down and started a family. Her dreams and expectations of a happily ever after were shattered after her 14 year marriage ended in divorce in 2012. This huge change was the catalyst she needed to began an internal journey resulting in freedom and peace. She published a book entitled *Bits & Pieces of a Broken Heart*, in which she shares her thoughts and struggles through her separation and divorce, as well as her decision to face the pain and grow. Her desire is to share her ongoing story of transformation from the prison of fear to the wide open space of love. She combines her passion for public speaking with her love of acting to create dramatic interpretations of her journey through a broken heart. She knows that every human being struggles to some degree with false beliefs, fear, loss and attachment. It is her desire to encourage and uplift, comfort and inspire those in the midst of their own battle. You can find her at www.spanishjanice.com.

JEALOUSY SITS IN MY BONES

By Janice Angela Burt

I see you and I feel it. Contempt, anger, jealousy.

I despise you and I don't even know you.

You are different than me. Different and beautiful and powerful.

And I hate you for it.

Seeing you standing there so poised, so confident, I immediately feel worthless, vulnerable, less than. You set off all my triggers with your perfection.

And if one other eye in this room focuses on you, I just might take out a few.

And yet, I smile politely and nod your way.

I act like you're not breaking my heart with every word you say.

I know that I'm creating my own little torture room, where jealousy, insecurity, and hate are there and in full bloom.

But I feel like I am driven from a place deep down inside, to resent you and reject you and then run away and hide.

It feels a curse to carry, it feels like an evil spell, this jealousy inside my heart I can see and taste and smell.

When I am controlled daily by my fears.

When failure is reflected in all the mirrors.

How do I step up and out from all these thoughts and all these doubts?

When I look at you and all I see are all the things that are wrong with me.

How do I change my path and leave behind the pain and wrath?

When my thoughts are negative at every turn and when love and trust seem hard to learn.

How do I transform my weary heart and exchange the past for a brand new start?

Hello and welcome to my mind! I have struggled with jealousy and insecurity since I was a teenager. This dynamic duo have been a fairly constant companion to me throughout this life's journey. They whisper in my ear telling me I'm not good enough. They say that I'll never measure up and that I'll be replaced by the next best and better, prettier and younger, bolder and brighter creature that comes along. And somehow, I believe their whisperings every single time.

When I was a teenager, I didn't feel comfortable in my feminine skin. I would rarely wear makeup and would dress in baggy clothes. Sex appeal frightened me. So I watched as my friends got all the looks and whistles from men, as well as their doting attention. Don't get me wrong, I also got attention from men.

However, my perception was that this attention was not because I was a gorgeous female externally, but because I was fun to hang out with and easy to talk to. Men were attracted to my insides, but I felt like I rated lower on the scale of external physical beauty. Because of this, I began to believe that I was not attractive enough, not pretty enough, not feminine enough, and ultimately, not good enough. I carried this belief system with me into my adult life, and there it has stayed and festered and poisoned in innumerable ways.

According to the ever-so-smart Wikipedia, jealousy is an emotion, and the word typically refers to the negative thoughts and feelings of insecurity, fear, and anxiety over an anticipated loss of something of great personal value, particularly in reference to a human connection.

This definition rings true to me. For as long as I can remember, I have had a fear of loss. When I was four and five years old my mom tells me that I would have a full on panic attack when she would walk out of the room to use the bathroom. I didn't want to be left alone. I had a fear that I would be abandoned, left behind forever. It turns out that mixing this fear of loss with the belief that I'm not good enough is a recipe for lots and lots of jealousy.

After yet another night where I allowed this jealousy to control me and affect the outcome of the evening, I sat down on my bed sobbing and hopelessly wrote the following:

Can jealousy sit in your bones?

Because I swear jealousy sits in my bones.

It sits and waits quietly, patiently, until that, there!

Some trigger sets it off.

And the jealousy gets restless from sitting so long in my bones.

It jumps to attention and gets ready for a full frontal attack.

It's sole intent is to destroy. To divide and conquer.

It is ruthless and takes no prisoners, annihilating everything in its path.

It leaves me feeling small and worthless and pathetic.

And then, once completely satiated, it settles back down and sits in my bones.

This is the ugly truth of my jealous tendencies. It feels so a part of me at times and so hard to escape, yet I am desperately searching for a solution. I don't like the woman I am when I let jealousy control me. Therefore, in the past year or so, I have been really paying attention, reading and researching about ways to combat this overpowering emotion.

By the way, the same could probably be used for any emotion that overpowers a person, such as anger, sadness, guilt, etc. Also, just so you know, I am writing this as one still in the trenches. I am wrestling and fighting with jealousy and insecurity as I type this. I am not writing from a place of victory, but from a place directly in the midst of the battle, bullets whizzing by me, grenade in my hand.

However, I am definitely more aware now than I used to be. I am very conscious of my own emotions, thoughts, and actions. When I feel jealous, I identify that I'm feeling jealous. I don't try to hide from it like I used to or deny it or minimize it. As a matter of fact, I would say that this is the first step toward any type of change you want to make in your life. Awareness. Nothing will or can change without it.

Before living my life from a place of awareness, I used to act like my pain and my fears did not exist. I would run from them, hide cleverly from them. It was a self protection mechanism that I used because I didn't think I could actually deal with the pain. I felt like the pain would certainly drown me and I would die from it. Yet I have discovered that the opposite is true. Sitting with my pain has actually been crucial to my healing. The following may be an old analogy, but it's a good one.

Imagine a huge infected wound on your arm. It's oozing and bleeding and hurts badly. You put a bandage over it and go about your day. The next day, the pain is worse and you start running a fever and almost faint. You decide to go to the emergency room and they have to cut into your arm and clean the wound deep down to treat the infection. The wound then begins to heal from the inside out. The same held true with my emotional pain. It hurt, so I didn't want to touch it. I didn't want to dig deep. Yet it was in the digging deep; it was in the painful moments that the infection was being cleared out. My inner self was being healed and my life would forever be transformed. It was so significant that I had to forgive myself for not doing it sooner. As a matter of fact, I had to forgive myself for numerous things...

As I went for an ordinary run on the river and extraordinary thing happened.

I forgave myself today.

I forgave myself for the years of allowing fear to control my steps.

I forgave myself for the victim mentality and always blaming someone else.

I forgave myself for giving up on me, for giving up on love.

I forgave myself for using different masks depending on what group I was a part of.

I forgave myself for keeping my true being locked up for so long.

I forgave myself for not allowing others to hear my own authentic song.

I forgave myself for living in denial and being too weak to choose to change.

I forgave myself for my desperate "love" and not seeking the tools to rearrange.

I forgave myself for whispering so many lies about my value and my worth.

I forgave myself for being too scared to speak up and speak out upon this earth.

I forgave myself for following unnecessary and unhealthy patterns set for me.

I forgave myself for loving those closest to me with so many conditions, now I see.

I forgave myself for lying and pretending just to feel good enough.

I forgave myself for all ways I've judged myself. Truth is, I've been pretty rough.

I forgave myself for unconscious living and so much deeply rooted fear.

I forgave myself for all the doubt and the emptiness I've held dear.

And after I forgave myself, I looked up in the sky to see

two eagles soaring overhead.

There they were, soaring wild and free.

And I knew then and I knew there that everything is simply how it's supposed to be.

Part of awareness is identifying our belief system. What do you believe about yourself?

Do you believe you are worthy?

Do you believe you are only as good as garbage?

Do you believe you are capable of magnificent feats?

Do you believe you will always live in a place of want and lack?

Do you believe you are strong and powerful?

Do you believe you are weak and ill equipped?

Do you believe you are better than everybody else?

Do you believe you are worse than everybody else?

The Change

What are your true, uncensored beliefs about yourself?

This is a time to be completely honest. Even if it hurts. It hurts my heart and makes me cringe inside to identify and say out loud that a good part of me believes that I am not good enough, not attractive enough, worthless. But the best thing I can do for myself is to be real in regard to my own heart and my own thoughts. There is something extremely powerful about embracing the emotions we feel and accepting that those are the feelings coursing through us in that particular moment. After one of my more difficult emotional days this past year, I wrote the following:

When I feel stuck and sad inside.

When all my instincts scream "Run! and hide!"

When life just seems off balance so

when the last thing I want to do is grow.

I allow myself to feel the ache.

I feel the unease that's hard to fake.

I allow myself just to be

wild, unsettled, and out of key.

I know inside that it's just a phase,

that life is about navigating this internal maze.

And little by little the burden and the pain

begin to evaporate like falling rain.

And I stand here feeling free once more

giving thanks for the past and the rest that's in store.

In this place of authenticity, there is hope for change and transformation; but if we're not willing to be honest with ourselves, we lock ourselves back up in the prison of our own fears and false beliefs.

It goes to reason that if the first step in transformation is identifying the belief systems we are operating under, then the next step would be to re-evaluate those belief systems. Ask ourselves why we believe the particular way we do. What happened in our childhood, in our adolescence, in our past that caused us to believe certain things about ourselves?

I've gone back in my past with the help of counseling, EMDR (Eye Movement Desensitization and Reprocessing), and hypnotherapy. I've discovered the instances, events, and circumstances that have created certain fears and false beliefs in me. It is a difficult, gut wrenching, yet absolutely essential process. It is imperative that we know the why of something so that we can combat and negate those false beliefs and fears when they creep back into our thoughts.

However, this is part of the process we should be very careful not to get stuck in! Human nature says it is much easier to blame than to accept responsibility. But at what point does this become OUR life?

We don't have control over everything that happens to us, but we do have control of our thoughts. Our thoughts dictate our emotions and actions. At some point, if we truly want to change, we must make a conscious choice to proceed differently than we have in the past. So now, instead of blaming, we can identify our false beliefs and our fears and then we let go of the past and take responsibility for our lives.

Sounds so easy, yet this simple step has proven to be the most difficult. Why do we feel the need to cling so desperately to our old, worn out beliefs and the horrible stories we tell ourselves about who we are? Why do I want to believe that I am ugly and not as good as the woman standing across the room from me? Why do we go back again and again to these negative cycles and these patterns that don't work? Possibly because letting go is hard to do. Even if it's letting go of a thought or belief that's holding us back or that makes us feel bad. It's just plain hard to let go.

Here are some tricks I use to help me let go of fears and false beliefs:

* **Yoga and running.** These two forms of exercise help me stay in the present moment and focus on the here and now. Also, there is a definite connection between feeling good physically and feeling good emotionally.

* **Replace my thoughts, and reason with myself.** When I am feeling jealous, I stop and reason with myself. I acknowledge the emotion of jealousy, but then I dig deeper and ask myself why I'm feeling jealous. I then realize that these feelings, although triggered by some external circumstance, come from a place inside of myself that feels less than and not good enough. I can then mentally negate those thoughts with the truth of my worth and the love that resides in me.

* **Take responsibility and create the life I want.** In other words, I take action! I was scared of expressing my own voice, so I joined Toastmasters and started giving speeches. I was scared of being vulnerable, so I published a book about my deepest thoughts and feelings. I was scared of failure, so I signed up to run a marathon to prove to myself that I could complete something difficult. There is no way to redo the past, but the present is sitting right in our lap, unwrapped, waiting to see what we're going to do with it. It is up to us to create the life we want!

* **Instill a gratitude mentality.** It's hard to be jealous and insecure when I'm feeling grateful for who I am and all that I have. Jealousy, as well as other negative emotions, abide in a dark, damp cave of negativity. Whereas gratitude abides in a field of wildflowers with blue skies all around it. We choose to live in either one or the other. We have the power of choice. Always.

* **Express what I'm feeling inside.** I write about it, talk about it, yell about it, cry about it, run about it, but one way or another I express my feelings. Repressing feelings does us no good. This is still a lesson that I'm learning because it has always been easier for me to live in denial. If I stuff it far enough down, it doesn't exist. Or so I thought. What I realized is that all those stuffed emotions are still there and I will never be able to expose and be rid of them unless I acknowledge them and see what it is they are trying to tell me.

Those are some of the changes that I've made in my own life to navigate my internal emotions and my fears. There are many more methods to use, but no matter what you use or how you do it, Just Do It! The change from living a life bound by fear to living a life free in love is one of the most beautiful transformations that can occur in this lifetime. If I do nothing in this life but encourage others to begin this process of transformation, I will die a happy and fulfilled woman.

This chapter has been a little difficult for me to write because it means really looking at my jealousy and insecurity. There is a pull on my ego when I think of people viewing me in this way, even if it's the truth. However, vulnerability has always proven to be a great asset. Being vulnerable means embracing myself, my whole being, flaws and all. Being vulnerable is a powerful key to transformation. My life has changed entirely for the better since I started being open and vulnerable with myself first, and then with others.

I will leave you with this final piece that I wrote when I was processing my decision to display the real me for all to see. Thank you for allowing me to share my heart and my journey with you. ♥

Exposed. Open. Bleeding still.

It feels so raw, being splayed open like this.

For all, for everyone to see

my pain, my scars.

Is it worth it?

Worth the feeling of rejection.

Of inferiority, of weakness.

I want to say no because of the pain,

but I know, I know

it's worth it.

As much as I want to hide and disappear,

it will always be

worth it.

Look at me, laugh at me, reject me, or mock me,

but I will still

remain

open.

For more information on Janice's work:

www.spanishjanice.com

bitsandpiecesbook.com

(916) 769-6394

MARY LYNN ZIEMER

After more than 25 years as a successful international senior executive with two Fortune 100 companies, and leading organizations ranging in size from 700 to 5,000, Mary Lynn now uses her unique skill set as a trendsetting entrepreneur, Certified Master Life and Business Coach, and Business Consultant. She is passionate about enhancing the quality of life for her clients, both professionally and personally. She helps people overcome roadblocks that may be preventing them from achieving dreams and goals.

Whether the goal is to create improved personal or business relationships, enjoy a better career/home balance, have more joy, feel more passion and purpose in life, increase financial wealth, or dramatically reduce stress and improve health, Mary Lynn is internationally known for her tools and techniques that help both individuals and organizations of all sizes achieve results.

In addition to her private coaching practice, Living A Joyful Life, Mary Lynn Ziemer is also a Coach and Mentor for 3Plus International. 3Plus International is a company that specializes in Coaching and Mentoring for aspiring professional women globally.

Mary Lynn is also an expert in "Emotional Intelligence," teaching people how to integrate feelings and thoughts (engaging in both the head and the heart) to create sustained performance and wellbeing, both professionally and personally. She inspires hearts and opens minds to leading edge new discoveries about how the brain works, using techniques that teach people to become positive, success-based thinkers. The tools that Mary Lynn teaches have been proven by Harvard University research to be more important than IQ and technical skills combined.

Additionally, as a renowned motivational speaker, Mary Lynn inspires audiences, sparks discussion, and motivates change. She is also a regular columnist on Wellness for the Gannett media company, with her work reaching audiences worldwide.

Mary Lynn's dynamic and authentic coaching style creates trust, motivates, and moves people toward positive change with tangible results. She assists her clients in finding their true purpose, then helps them create and achieve goals around that purpose. Mary Lynn Ziemer unveils the secrets of life that "we were never taught in school." She provides useful tools for creating perfect health, amazing personal and professional relationships, and finding true joy in all aspects of life.

EVOLVING YOU

Embrace Happiness to Create the Life of Your Dreams

By Mary Lynn Ziemer

"Happiness is not a state to arrive at, but a manner of traveling." - Margaret Lee Runbeck

The eternal search for happiness... it's a human condition. For many, happiness is something they are constantly chasing, but never attaining. For others, they understand that happiness and overwhelming joy are readily available at anytime, anywhere... despite circumstance.

Wherever you are on your journey, it is possible for you to have a life filled with more joy... right now! How can you do this? On the surface, the answer may seem huge and illusive. It may feel like it could take your entire life to make this kind of shift. But in reality, it is quite simple.

Happy people use specific strategies that allow them to feel a sense of control over their lives. They wake to each new day with plans to *create* the life they want, not simply "discover" it. They feel empowered to *make* it the best day possible.

No matter who you are or what you do, you can choose to have the life that you want. But in order to be successful, you must first be happy. Happiness is the precursor to success. It does not work the other way around. True happiness in every aspect of your life is possible, you just have to wrap your mind around it.

First, *know* that you have the power to create your life in any way you want it to be! We have unlimited potential beyond our wildest dreams. Albert Einstein was considered one of the most brilliant people to have ever lived. However, science tells us that he used only 10% of his brain. Even as Einstein died, he knew that he had not scratched the surface of the power of the mind.

Over the past 20 years, Harvard University has conducted psychological studies of the minds of 275,000 people. The results concluded that *everything* is improved when your brain experiences high levels of happiness. In fact, it has been proven that happiness leads to success in every domain of our lives: marriage, health, friendship, community involvement, creativity, income, jobs, careers, and businesses.

So, just imagine what is waiting for you as you begin to tap into even more of that power of your mind, which starts with being happy. You can grow and change in ways you never expected. You can realize the life you truly desire.

Here's how to get started.

Have a positive mindset

Know the power of your thoughts, and constantly replace negative thoughts with better feeling thoughts. In other words, "flip the switch." Do this consciously and intentionally all day long.

Everything that has ever been created in your life began with a thought! While your thoughts are the basis of your intention (your dreams and goals), it is the emotion tied to these thoughts that actually does the creating. That's why being happy is the basis for having the life of your dreams. It is never too late or too early to begin.

Focus on what you want, not on what you don't want. We have an average of 50,000 to 80,000 thoughts a day, so many of which are negative thoughts from our past or worries about our future. When you learn to focus more and more on what you want right now you'll begin to see a shift in how you feel and what you are creating for yourself.

"Flip the Switch" consistently for fast results:

It is imperative that you learn to "flip the switch" consistently in order to master your life. Try this method 3 to 5 times a day to get you started. The more often you are able to "flip the switch," the better. Remember, the goal is to feel better at the end of the exercise than you did when you began. So, take note at the end and have gratitude for your newfound feelings of peace, or for the burst of joy that you experience.

Action Plan:

Below is a journaling exercise. After doing this for 21 days, it will become second nature. You won't even need to write it down any longer, as you will be consistently in touch with what you are feeling and why you feel that way. To get started though, it is best to set the alarm or reminder on your phone to sound multiple times a day to remind you to journal. This will get you going and keep you on track.

Find a quiet, private space where you can write down your answers. Don't wait another minute! Schedule your alarm right now. Do this consistently, and it's guaranteed that you will feel better fast. You will open the door to unlimited possibilities.

Each time you write in your journal, answer these three questions.

Q 1) "How do I feel right now?" Close your eyes, tap into your feelings, and be honest with yourself. Use words of emotion to describe what you feel, such as happy, stressed, frustrated, joyful, or peace in your heart and body. Take a few deep breaths to calm your mind. Write it down.

If you tap into a moment when you are feeling great, follow-through with the exercise and complete it with the intent of feeling *even better* at the end than you did when you started.

Q 2) Close your eyes again and ask yourself, "What am I thinking about right now that is making me feel this way?" Be quiet within yourself and write whatever comes to your mind. It may be a paragraph or a sentence. Just write until you feel you have the root cause of your feelings.

Q 3) Get quiet and ask yourself, "What can I think about right now that will make me feel (even) better? This is where the "flipping the switch" technique comes in.

For example, if someone in your life has upset you by treating you less than kindly, try writing something like this: I am so grateful that (person's name) always treats me with respect. He/she is always kind and caring.

Please note that while this statement may initially feel like a lie, in order for your new belief to take hold, you must repeat the thought over and over again. Here's why.

Remember the age-old adage "a lie told over and over again eventually becomes the truth?" Harvard studies show conclusively that the beliefs we hold become our self-fulfilling prophecy over time. These reversed statements are "good lies" for the moment, so enjoy the prospect of them coming true and they will! A "belief" is simply a thought repeated over and over again. As you practice a new way of thinking, your new belief will take hold to get the result you want. Consistency is key!

This method has worked for people over and over again. If you want to see some real life examples, visit LivingAJoyfulLifeNow.com and check out reviews of clients who have shared their experiences through written or video messages.

In one of these reviews, a recent young client shared how she changed a long-time negative and painful relationship with her sister simply by employing this technique.

She changed the view of her sister to one that she really wanted. Her new version of her sister made her feel good to think about and write out so she did it often throughout the day. She especially practiced this when negative thoughts of her sister entered her mind. She would write, "I am so grateful that my sister and I have a close loving relationship. We have fun together wherever we are and she treats me with respect always."

In *less than one week*, this client changed how her older sister treated her. It's now been only 2 months since she made the change and their relationship is one of great friendship, fun, and joy.

When it comes to anything in your life - relationships, circumstances, money, no matter what - the only thing that holds you back from having the life of your dreams is you, your negative thoughts and feelings, limiting beliefs and the drama you unknowingly create in your life.

For every aspect of your life that you do not like, with absolute certainty, you will find limiting beliefs (with negative feelings attached) at the root of the problem, But the good news is this - all you have to do is identify the belief that doesn't feel good. Once you've identified it, change it to a love based belief, write it as an affirmation (example above) that makes you feel happy, and repeat the thought over and over again. This retrains your mind to believe a new and better feeling thought, which then gets you the end you're dreaming of.

Know that it is possible to change everything, *yes everything*, with focused feelings of love and belief that everything can happen just the way you want it to.

Because you get what you expect, believe, and feel, you must understand how you are feeling first to make the process work. Over time, the scale will tip in your favor. You will see evidence of your new dominant thoughts and feelings showing up in your reality. When you do, be sure to note the changes you see and write a statement of gratitude for them at the end of your day. Keep these statements of gratitude in a journal and refer back to them for uplifting mental reinforcement when you need it. This will surely bring you even more to be grateful for!

Unleash your Imagination

Get crystal clear about your goals and have unwavering faith. Expand the power of your imagination by asking yourself what you really want. Do you know? If not, ask for clarity. For example, "I am so grateful that I have clarity about my dream job now."

Again, try a little journaling and just dream about who you want to be, want you want to do and what you'd like to have. This list should represent your ideal life, one where you shoot for the universe, not just the moon or stars. Don't give any consideration to how you will make these dreams come true, as that will simply interrupt the flow of your inspired thoughts and creativity.

Before you start this process, get calm and quiet. Stop analyzing, and shift to that part of your mind where all of your creative power lies… just waiting to be unleashed. Write a free-flowing list of everything you want to be, do, and have, without putting any limits on yourself about how is it possible. Don't worry about knowing how you will do it or whether or not you deserve it. Just let it flow and know that you have the power of faith within you to make your dreams come true.

Don't wait another moment. Get started now!

Write down the goals you've defined. According to Harvard research, this will speed up the manifestation process by as much as 1000%! Identify what keeps you from believing you can reach the outcome you want, then acutely focus on the opposite.

Develop a list of affirmations and create new beliefs that serve you well, make you feel great, and allow you to redirect your precious energy to focus solely on what you want.

Next, take inspired action toward reaching your goals. Ask yourself what you can do *right now,* from where you are, with what you have, to make it happen - and get started immediately. Don't worry about how big or small the action is. Just show the Universe and God that you are committed to doing your part, and more opportunity will come your way. As each new opportunity presents itself, follow-through using your internal GPS, your inner voice, to guide you.

Always follow your gut instinct and it will lead you to your truth!

Love Yourself Intensely

Let's talk about the necessity of self-love, not to be confused with arrogance or narcissism. These traits have nothing to do with *love.*

First you need to know how special and unique you are. Know who you really are and embrace your uniqueness. Get clear about what you want out of your life, what your gifts, talents, joys and passions are, and pursue them. Relentlessly. We are all unique and our belief systems are different, so do not compare yourself to anyone else. Focus only on comparing yourself to your own growth. How much are you growing into the unique and talented person that you are?

Love yourself unconditionally, knowing that you are creating your world based on how you feel. Make self-care your number #1 priority, and others around you will benefit from your overflowing "love tank." Remember that if you don't feel intense love for you, making good personal choices at every turn, your love tank will be empty. You can't give to others what you don't have. You may try, but it becomes quickly evident when your love tank is empty.

Know that within your heart you hold all that is good. Begin to see the beauty within you, and you will also begin to see the beauty all around you and in others. Your world is simply a reflection of what you hold for yourself inside. If you judge yourself at any level, at any time, you will surely be judgmental of others. This judgment creates negativity, drama and frustration.

Elevate your self-talk to radiate your loving energy outward. Whatever you tell yourself inside your head, day in and day-out, becomes the reality of your world around you. When you change your own inner dialogue to unconditional self-love, you are safe, accepted, and loved. When you think only loving thoughts of others, you expand that love even further.

When you love yourself, you are able to see your own perfection, regardless of where you are in your life right now. You will also find it easier to accept and love others for who they are. You will see only their perfection and beauty, and understand that they are perfectly on their path, just as you are.

Move yourself toward peace and calm.

Calm is the key. The more you grow in self-love the more your calm will increase and you will consistently connect to that inner voice of wisdom that is within you. Be diligent about building quiet time into your schedule daily to meditate, pray, or relax in silence. Living in the zone of calm provides more benefits than you can imagine. The endless possibilities are only limited by your imagination.

Calm allows you to see the perfection in others, treating them with the kindness, respect, and honor that we should afford to ourselves as well. Loving others unconditionally is a direct result of loving ourselves. You'll also gain faith of a certainty that all is possible; and you'll find the joy of the present moment easier to experience with the patience of knowing beyond a doubt, that what you want is already on its way.

Calm comes from deep happiness and joy. So as you build your foundation of self-love and gratitude, you will *become* love.

Have FUN!

Fun is always a choice - and usually the *right* choice! There is always a way to change whatever you are doing into something that you find more fun. When you shift your attitude, then add your imagination and love to the mix, it is not only possible... but shockingly easy. It may just be as simple as adding a smile. A smile or a good laugh always feels great, and love is always the shortcut to fun!

The secret to having fun is to reframe your day, moment by moment, based on how you feel. Know that when your feelings are off, your thoughts are always far from positive as well. So the trick lies in shifting your thoughts and actions once again, to finding the positive in that moment. Get right down to a basic view of gratitude for whatever it is that you are focused on at the moment. Fun is just a thought or idea or picture away!

Have incredible and endless gratitude.

Be grateful for everything that you already have in your life, big or small. Give thanks all day long, living in the present moment… appreciating yourself, everyone and everything else. Know that constant gratitude will more easily bring you more to be grateful for. Without an "attitude of gratitude" you block the flow of abundance. Relive the wonderful feelings of gratitude by writing them down at the end of your day. Create a gratitude journal to revisit them frequently and fill your love tank all over again.

Live consciously using these steps, and your happiness and joy will soar to heights yet unachieved. The evolution of your personal power and the use of your mind will far exceed your expectations. Then, watch as God and the Universe bring you everything you request. Know that love is the power and the answer to everything!

To learn more about Mary Lynn Ziemer, including her articles, Blogs, and other tips for joyful living, visit www.LivingAJoyfulLifeNow.com or call (239) 498-7290.

The Change

KAREN MARSHALL

There is nothing run-of-the-mill about life when you are on a spiritual path. This has been true for Karen Marshall, especially since learning about the Law of Attraction. She is still a work in progress and expects to be progressing and expanding as long as she is on the planet.

A long-time student of metaphysics, she had experienced more loss in her life than most people have. Coming from a dysfunctional background, she was always seeking ways to better understand herself.

Having been trained in several different healing modalities, she had not found the process that she wanted to work with. When she heard about, and experienced for herself, the Pulse Technique, she knew that this was the process that would bring an inner sense of purpose and fulfillment, and also offer life transforming processes for her clients.

Her major accomplishments have come since she learned to stop living life in reverse. These accomplishments include authoring the newly released transformational book *Atom & Even*, and acquiring training in the powerful Quantum Pulse clearing processes that she facilitates and offers through her website.

THE GOLDEN ERA

By Karen Marshall

The year 2012 left many people fearful that the world might come to an end, others stocking supplies for natural or human-made disasters, and still others thinking it was a bunch of foolishness.

As it turned out, it was, indeed, the end. Not the end of the world, but the end of an era. What we are experiencing right now is a new beginning in the Golden Era.

We are all going through an awakening process; awakening to the divinity that we are and the freedom of the choices that we have. We have been described as beautiful butterflies emerging from our chrysalis.

For some, things have taken off in grand new ways, for others it is their time of greatest struggle, and for still others it is business as usual, unaware of the changes that are taking place on the planet.

Thomas Kuhn, author of *The Structure of Scientific Revolutions*, physicist and philosopher of science said, "Think of a Paradigm Shift as a change from one way of thinking to another. It's a revolution, a transformation, a sort of metamorphosis. It does not just happen, but rather it is driven by agents of change."

There are many terms associated with what is taking place. First, we have moved into the Age of Aquarius at the same time we are ascending in consciousness. This Ascension is also called the Awakening, as we are all waking up and shifting into the oneness that is part of the new Golden Era and the fourth and fifth dimensions of consciousness. This might sound confusing, but it is unfolding incrementally, though at a rather rapid pace.

The Mayan calendar, which came to an end in 2012, corresponds with the Mayan cosmic pyramid at Bolon Yokte Ku, which has nine steps. Each step has a certain wave or frequency of energy attached to it.

We have completed the ninth step.

9th step, 234 days

8th step, 12.8 years

7th step, 256 years

6th step, 5,125 years

5th step, 102,000 years

4th step, 2,050,000 years

3rd step, 41,000,000 years

2nd step, 820,000,000 years

1st step, 16,400,000,000 years to complete

Carl Johan Calleman, author of *Solving the Greatest Mystery of Our Time: The Mayan Calendar*, says:

> "The 9th and highest step on the pyramid propels a process that leads the universe and human beings to their highest state of consciousness and will result in a timeless, cosmic consciousness, and a citizenship in the universe, on the part of humanity. The

ninth wave was to cap the entire evolution of the universe that, so far, had been propelled by the eight lower waves of the previous steps on the pyramid. From what is known about the changing polarities of consciousness of the nine waves, it will do so by providing energies that are conducive to the human beings co-creating unity consciousness."

****

The 16.4 billion years depicted by the pyramid might seem unrealistic, but we can see by the progression of evolution in terms of our known history, that moving from the one-celled amoeba to our present state of being had to take a great deal of time. According to Time.com, the first known dinosaurs lived 243 million years ago.

In the history of the earth, nearly all living matter was destroyed by natural disasters on five separate occasions. This time however, we, the inhabitants of Earth, have been given the opportunity to see the earth rise to a higher level without having to damage the planet and begin again. Human vibration and consciousness has risen to the degree that we can assist in this process, while inhabiting the planet, as we move into the Golden Era.

Each step on the pyramid brought with it an increase in the frequency vibration 20 times greater than the previous step. There was also a speed-up of time with each step to the next higher level. These higher frequency waves of energy, which are still coming, have intensified astronomically since ascending the last step on the pyramid. The energies are transforming our minds and our bodies so that we can handle the higher frequencies. This energy affects all life on the planet and the planet itself.

It is said that each and every one of us chose to be here on the planet at this time. We were brought forth from the pool of souls awaiting the opportunity to come to the planet to experience the richness of growth that can be achieved here. The growth and expansion that is now taking place on the planet is unprecedented, as the earth and its inhabitants are being raised to higher levels of consciousness and vibration.

This is a marvelous time to be on the planet, for nothing like this has ever been done before. All will be experiencing this exciting transformation as the earth moves away from the density, duality, and drama of the third dimension into the love, light, and oneness of the fourth and fifth dimensions.

HeartMath, an internationally recognized nonprofit research and education organization, estimates that about 20 percent of the world's population is actively involved in various ways to help achieve this transformation. Those who are participating are attempting to accelerate the process by consciously doing the inner work of clearing their energy fields of all unwanted thoughts, beliefs, and attitudes that hinder them from moving forward. By doing so they are raising their own vibration and consciousness, in addition to that of the collective and of the planet itself, as all are connected.

The veils of forgetfulness that descended on us at birth are being lifted. During our first six years of life, the accumulation of other peoples' input in the form of imprinting, subconscious programs, and limiting core beliefs, caused us to separate from our true, authentic self, our soul, creating the thickening of the veil.

The membrane, or veil of separation, is getting thinner as new ways of being and perceiving are showing up. We will no longer be seeing through the glass darkly.

Jo Dunning, developer of Quantum Energetic Disciplines, says:

> "The mind has been in charge and the ego has been directing it. The ego has been one of the tools that have helped us to create in the world. It has given us motivation, inspiration, direction, and often correction when we have encountered certain events in the world.
>
> We created our identity and attached ourselves to the external ways and acknowledgments that we received in the world. All of this relates to the lower three chakras and the 3D world. We are now

completing that process in our evolution as we move up into the higher charkas and higher states of consciousness."

****

Once we completed the ninth and last step of the pyramid, the door to the third dimension was closed. We moved into the higher frequencies of the fourth and fifth dimensions.

Jim Self, channel of Teachers of Light and coauthor of *What Do You Mean the Third Dimension is Going Away?*, suggests that some aspects of the third dimension remain close at hand - those of thoughts, beliefs, and habits - but these will begin to dissipate once we make the decision to let go of them and begin functioning from the higher realms.

Now, functioning from the fourth and fifth dimensions, as our vibration rises, we become immune to emotional dramas taking place around us. Such behaviors will simply no longer hold our interest.

Dimensions are not places; dimensions are states of consciousness. We did not go *someplace*, we are becoming *something* new - a new state of consciousness.

As the lower three chakras are cleared of distorted notions of the self and the accumulated emotional baggage we've been carrying, these lower chakras will no longer be a part of our reality. As individuals begin the work of recovering the essence of whom they are at their core, they become less connected to, influenced by, or affected by 3D remnants.

Richard Barrett, international thought leader and author of *What My Soul Told Me* and *Spiritual Unfoldment: A Guide to Liberating Your Soul*, explains:

> "Physical awareness is three-dimensional, soul awareness is of the fourth dimension. Three-dimensional awareness has the basic qualities of time, space and matter. These qualities create the experiences of separation, death and mass.
>
> Fourth dimension is soul awareness, having the basic qualities of timelessness, spacelessness and energy. These qualities create the

experiences of unity, being, and flow. In the fourth dimension, there is consciousness of eternity, where past and future simultaneously co-exist. There is consciousness of omnipresence, in which everywhere is located right here. In other words, the here and now is "Home Central" of the fourth dimension. There is a sense in the here and now of a permanent sense of being. That being is not of things, but of energy. In the fourth dimension of consciousness there is only an eternal moment that we call now and everything exists in energy forms.

The emotion of fear and a fixation on external circumstance are symptoms of attachment to the 3-D world. Love is an expression of the fourth, a shared awareness with all energy forms of our essential unity. Intention is the secret of navigating in this realm. Most important is for us to look for our soul's intention behind every experience, to see what we are trying to learn. In the final analysis, the most important lesson is that our ideals become our destiny."

****

Once your soul has expanded, regardless of your age or what you feel is pulling you inward to get to the essence of who you really are, or pushing you outward to experience more of the world, there is no turning back. You are moving into wakefulness, for the slumber we have been experiencing will no longer suffice.

The deeper we delve within, opening and clearing the passageways of the soul, the greater is our alignment with our own divine self and with the Divine Itself. In the process, our natural abilities and freedoms return to us along with wonderful new freedoms and abilities.

It is a huge undertaking to change the consciousness and the vibration of the entire world population, but every step forward in the raising of consciousness, by any one person, is a gift to the whole. This highly intense energy that is now available, is assisting us in clearing out that which no longer serves us.

The unwanted energies that are within our energy field and the cells and atoms of our body are being pushed to the surface by these incoming, planetary energies - where they can now, more easily, be recognized and cleared. As the unwanted energies are released, our vibration rises and our consciousness expands.

It might feel that you are pushing your own buttons so that you can get on with it and move into the higher levels of thinking, feeling, and being. What might have been an uncomfortable "norm" for you in past situations or circumstances might now feel intolerable. Add to that the speed in time and you might be feeling a sense of urgency to rid yourself of anything that holds you back from all that you are.

There could be some confusion as this process is unfolding, for it might still feel like having one foot in the third dimension (the dense, logical, structured world) and the other foot in the fourth dimension (the light, magical, mystical world). This could make anyone's head spin.

The transformation that is taking place within each of us is simultaneously taking place within the planet. The same cleansing process is occurring on all levels: microcosm and macrocosm. Just as the planet has been experiencing earthquakes, floods, tsunamis, and fires, so too have countries been experiencing disruptions in politics, economy, education, healthcare, food and water sources, energy supplies, and the weighty stand as to which nation is now the mightiest.

On the personal level, it goes to the core of our being, bringing into clear view anything that is disrupting the natural flow of energy in our body and our life, whether it is in relationships, finances, health, employment, or our perception of the planet as a whole. Any and all areas that the soul can use to get our attention will be used, as we are called on to do our inner work. The clearing of unresolved issues is necessary, for we cannot take our emotional baggage with us on this journey into the higher realms.

With the ninth and final step, at the top of the pyramid, taking only 234 days as opposed to 16.4 billion years of the first step, is it any wonder that we are experiencing this dramatic speed up of time?

The acceleration of time applies not only to what we can or cannot seem to accomplish in a day but also to the speed of our consciousness. Today it is difficult to keep up with the new innovations in technology, as new products appear before one has learned to operate, at full functioning, the previous new model. Yes, technology is moving at a rapid pace, but so is the consciousness of those who are creating these new, improved models.

Our consciousness is on a fast track and getting faster day-by-day. This acceleration of consciousness is not just being used for material inventions but also for the creative use of the mind and how to activate the laws of the universe to bring on the life that we desire. There are mighty forces behind this movement and Infinite Consciousness is leading the way of this expansion into consciousness and the rapid pace of the planet.

****

In the third dimension, we depended on our five senses to determine our reality. In the fourth dimension we will depend on our heart-based knowing, our intuition, and other extrasensory skills for that determination.

Telepathy, channeling, healing, and psychic abilities are on the rise, and our ability to manifest is now easier and faster than ever before. As our knowing expands, our capabilities and creativity, in all areas, will increase, making things doable that we thought before were impossible.

The fourth dimension is the point between the third dimension (physical reality) and the fifth dimension (spiritual reality). As such, the fourth dimension corresponds to the heart (fourth) chakra, which is the point between the lower three chakras, related to the physical realm, and the higher three chakras, related to the spiritual realm.

The fourth dimension shares the energy of love with the heart chakra, and both are fully available to us now. As more of the energy of love opens to us, or emanates from us, it allows unconditional love and forgiveness to permeate our lives and to heal the wounds of our past.

There are four levels to the fourth dimension. The first level is a little difficult to traverse, as it contains every thought that has ever been thought that did not manifest. It can have a thick, gummy feel to it. As you pass through this level, it might feel that your thoughts are not your own, that they are being imposed on you, or that the thoughts are thinking you.

The highest, or fourth level, is as heaven on earth. Howard Martin of HeartMath says that the majority of the world population is about mid-level fourth dimension at this time.

And what about the fifth dimension? The fourth dimension is the world of magic, the fifth dimension is the world of miracles. Both are fully in place and occupied; the fourth by most people and the fifth by some people.

It is the fifth dimension that we are aiming for, but we have to master our emotions before we can make that shift. The fourth dimension is the area where we have the opportunity to experience our thoughts and emotions fully so that we can make the necessary adjustments to master them.

The fastest route to living and being in the fourth level of the fourth dimension is to do your inner work, clean up your emotional act, and set your soul free.

Where to start? Stop mentally or verbally telling your stories of troubling or unresolved issues. These keep you stuck in a low, dense vibration. Tell a whole new, expanded story of how you would like things to be. Don't base your new story on happenings from the past. Create something brand new.

Vital to this shift is to love yourself - all of you - body, mind, and soul. Try not to compare yourself to others. You are uniquely individual.

Next, don't fall victim to anything or anybody who you feel resistance to. Victim mentality is rampant on this planet of people pleasers. When you go into victim mode, you abandon yourself, causing separation within yourself and that does not correspond to the oneness that the planet is moving toward.

And finally, be in the present moment as much as possible. Now is where all the action is and where creation starts. In the fourth dimension, now is the only time that exists. The only place that you will find the presence of God, Source Energy, is in the present. Meditate your way into the now.

As you expand into the Golden Era, you will experience a heightened state of awareness, a higher state of consciousness, and you will be vibrating at a higher frequency. You will master the emotions that have kept you slave to the 3D world, uncover the divinity that you are, and feel a deeper connection with Infinite Intelligence as you plumb the depths of your own being.

We all work at our own pace and advance accordingly. As we move to higher dimensions, we become fearless, limitless, and spiritually awakened. We are all becoming a new way of being. We are multidimensional beings living in a multidimensional universe.

This time has been prophesized and predicted for centuries by many, and it's time has now come. It has been described as 1,000 years of peace.

May you all have a blessed journey!

If you would like a more joyful, connected, and gratifying life, you can learn more at:

www.5thdimensionhealingenergy.com

This chapter includes excerpts from the book *Atom & Even*, available at Amazon.com.

The Change

STACI BOYER

Staci Boyer is an award winning published Author, a Pride nutrition sponsored Bikini Athlete, Master Trainer with a Master of Fitness Sciences certified through the ISSA & ACE, and holds a BA in Social Sciences. She is a fitness educator, motivational speaker, fitness competitor and mother of 2!

Her experiences span from 12 years as an active duty Navy Hospital Corpsman to over 26 years in the fitness industry as a personal trainer, fitness media representative for WGN, NBC, CBS, and FOX, and group exercise instructor and General Manager for a leading health club chain. Now owning her own business, Motiv8nU™ and fitness competition team, Team Motiv8nU Elite, she is passionately building a fit and driven community that focuses on a well rounded healthy life of generosity and hard work! #Motiv8nu4REAL

MOTIV8N'U

To Be Your Own Game Changer

By Staci Boyer

Finding and harnessing your inner strength to propel you to become a champion change maker. Since I can remember I have been told stories of Samson and Delilah. The heated desire Samson had for the beautiful Delilah and the hidden strength that gave Samson his mystery for the ages. Songs have been written - and believe me I have sung a few in my day - telling this historical tale. What draws me more to the story isn't just the heated sex and betrayal between the two, but more in the strength and power associated with Samson's long hair.

I have often used the comparison when poking fun at my own need to be in constant sync with the care and nurturing of my own tresses. But at the end of the day, my well groomed head of hair does dictate the pep in my step, not to mention the power in every move I make. Whether down, or in my signature bun, every lock represents to me where I have been, and more importantly, where I am going.

We all have something in our lives that gives us that pep, that extra mojo, the extra push we need to harness our inner game changer. Clark Weber tells us that "everything you want is just on the other side of fear." Now let us explore the power that is within us all - the power that will help take us to that other side and create the change we all so desperately seek.

I am a game changer, I am a change maker, I ride the wave of change and I will not be sucked under it. How do I know this? Because I looked in the mirror, directly into my own eyes, and I said those words out loud. I made those words real.

Somewhere along my life path however, I must have been taught the importance of this philosophy; the importance of embracing change, and not fearing it. It is not an easy feat mind you. The path of least resistance can be a much easier road to travel with less obstacles less road blocks, and certainly less fear.

However, at the end of the day I can assure you, far less reward will be found there as well. We often tread in the comfort zone, fearing the unknown yet scared of what is in front of us. What exactly is in front of us? Look in the mirror. What do you see? Who do you see? STOP for a moment and write down 5 great things that you see. STOP yourself from finding flaw or negativity. Do not even go there. You may see a beautiful smile or sparkling eyes. You may notice a strong confident jaw line or an artistic arch in your eyebrow. You many even close your eyes and simply be, and find strength and peace in that silence. Any and all of these things are windows into the very soul and fiber of your very own game changer. Once you identify the strengths that you posses, you can own them and use them to harness your power to make any changes you seek in your life.

The difference between being self referenced and object referenced is a huge factor in your ability to be the master of your domain, so to speak. Deepak Chopra teaches that allowing our emotions to be controlled by outside forces or people and not by our own intrinsic motivators will lead us down a confusing disgruntled path. So find your strengths, accept them, and embrace them. Deepak Chopra also tells us "to find that place inside yourself where nothing is impossible." I encourage you to allow your own emotions and motivators - not others - to dictate your actions and create change.

Let us talk about fear. Your destiny is not by chance, it is by choice. Through choice we make change. The human condition is to be uncertain of choices and thereby be fearful of change. We must first change this mindset to move forward. Fear is defined as an "unpleasant emotion caused by the belief that someone or something is dangerous, likely to cause pain, or a threat." Now if we decide to break down this definition and dissect emotion, we have a "natural instinctive state of mind deriving from one's circumstances, mood, or relationships with others." (Oxford) The operative words here are one's and others. This tells us that emotion - in this case fear - is owned by us, and therefore ultimately controlled by us. Great news right? Well, then the word others comes into play. This is where we have to say "I will be SELF referenced," as in, "I OWN my emotions," and not be OBJECT referenced, and thereby controlled or swayed by the actions of OTHERS.

Must I take this a step further you ask? Why, indeed I shall! Going back to our original definition of fear, we find the word belief. Oxford defines belief as "something one accepts as true or real; a firmly held opinion or conviction." How about that! I see that operative word one again! What does this even mean? Well, it means that yet again… WE have control. We have the reins. We are at the helm. We have the con. WE my friends are always the master of our domain… if we want to be.

Ok, lets piece together this fear framework and how it affects our ability to change, or in other words, NOT change. Every thing and every change we want in life is on the other side of fear. We must learn to find our way around that fear, to harness it, and to push it aside. Fear is a manifested emotion that we are in control of. We have complete ownership and responsibility for our emotions.

Remember, our emotion must be self referenced, NOT object referenced. Do not allow others to dictate your emotion - period. This will only fuel your fear and hold back change. Finally, when you believe with conviction that you and only you are the master of your domain and controller of your emotion - and firmly stand in the strength that is you and only YOU - fear will be faced head on.

Remember earlier when I said to look in the mirror and find 5 positive things. These are 5 things that fuel your strength, NOT your fear. LOOK straight into the mirror - recognize and own those things AND your strength. Use that strength to look around the fear, own your emotion and become your own change maker! When I glance back one last time before I leave the house and check my red hair, I'm really solidifying my power in my ability to stare fear in the face, push it aside, look around it and achieve the change I seek. I want to teach you how to make this a reality for you. Everything we do is a process. Consistency is key. Time over tension... I could go on and on. Point being - you will not become unafraid overnight.

You may even stare in the mirror blankly for days and not come up with 5 game changer powers at all. The first day you may actually find 5 flaws. The second day maybe 2. Then you may look and see nothing great - but nothing bad either. THEN... TA-DA! It WILL happen. One by one, your amazing gifts will appear, I promise you. We all travel down the road of LOW SELF ESTEEM or I'M WORTHLESS, more than once in our lifetime. I can assure you there are some locals along my low road that recognize me when they see me coming from a distance. However, over the years we have become friendly - as I have traveled this road too often. And they thankfully have re-named my old bar from, THIS IS THE LIFE to KEEP YOUR ASS MOVING - The corner of work & hustle is just up ahead!

Real talk. It happens. It happens again. We start recognizing when it happens, and more importantly why it happens. The secret here is this.... are you ready? EVERY single time, and I do mean EVERY single time things seem to be at their worst, it means life is about to get amazing. This is the life circle. The trick is to recognize that it is happening. Sadly most people cannot. If you took the looking in the mirror and finding your 5 secret powers activity seriously, you my friend are now armed and dangerous! This is the first step in knowing that things get bad but they WILL always get better; AND more importantly, we have complete control of the process. The secret powers help... or as I fondly call them, My 3 secret assassin moves. Yes, this of course includes something to do with my red hair!

There was a time in my life when I strolled leisurely on the I'M WORTHLESS Highway. I didn't even pitch a tent, I pathetically unrolled my tattered sleeping bag in the crevice of an underpass - like a hobo - and thought someone would save me. I actually cut off my hair. Probably in an attempt to hurt myself or find myself. Who knows. Thankfully, one day I remembered who I really was, when I looked into a dirty gas station mirror - the kind that is more like a fun house mirror - and saw my weakness where I had once recognized strength. It took years to get my hair back but only one moment to remember the strong woman I actually was. Everything is a journey. Everything is a process. My hair is still growing. I do not own that tattered sleeping bag anymore, yet I have visited the underpass. The locals on my old frequented path of destruction that see me coming from a distance - but only once in a while - they always point out the new name of the bar and comment on my beautiful long red hair.

We need to make your game-changing action plan.

Action Steps

Step 1 - Identify your fear - write it down

Step 2 - Identify your game changer powers - write them down

Step 3 - Accept them, own them, say what they are out loud while looking at yourself in the mirror - every day for 7 days.

Step 4 - Set goals that will steer you toward what you were once fearful of according to MOTIV8NU THE BOOK- *see attached template and breakdown

Step 5 - ON day 8 take the paper you wrote your fear on and burn it - yep... burn it

Step 6 - Refer back to goal break down and BEGIN

Step 7 - Revaluate every 30 days

Step 8 - Continuously look fear head on - close your eyes - become one with your game changer powers and step around fear - outside of your comfort zone

Evaluate these areas of your life

- Financial – 401k – insurance - savings
- Functional – closet – kitchen - garage
- Friends & Family - parents – friends - spouse
- Focused / Vocational - work
- Feeling/Emotional – feelings about "things"
- Witness the Fitness / Spiritual wellness – Church?
- Feeding your fitness /Nutrition – Clean eating
- Funny Bone Fitness – Laugh at yourself

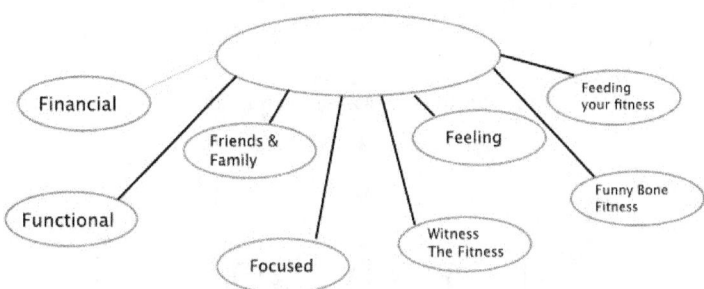

In the BIG blank circle - Write down one big long term goal that you have for yourself.
It can be anything from loosing 30 pounds to finishing a Doctorate!

Take a moment and think about
What YOU need to do to make positive change and achieve goals
in each of the smaller circles···
if anything···

The Change

Financial	Functional	Friends & Family	Focused	Feeling	Witness The Fitness	Feeding your fitness	Funny Bone Fitness

List 4 things to do to work on each goal.

This Months Plan!

Pick one thing from each of the four that you wrote down for each goal. These are the 8 things that you will clearly focus on for the next 30 days.

Financial	Functional	Friends & Family	Focused	Feeling	Witness The Fitness	Feeding your fitness	Funny Bone Fitness

What happens here is that you are able to focus on the parts of your life that you know you need to address. It may be something simple like cleaning out your closet, or calling your mother… but I promise you, the weight that will be lifted off of you will give you confidence you need to make your way around your fear, outside of your comfort zone and make the change you seek. Life is a process.. As you know – but here is a great way for YOU to take charge of this process!

"Strength is not defined by the absence of moments of weakness, but more in our ability to overcome those moments." Boyer

Two elementary schools, two middle schools, and four high schools - a lot of changes.

I drank a lot. I did some drugs. I don't anymore - I changed.

I was raped. I was depressed. I hated myself. I hated everyone. I don't anymore - I am changed.

I allowed myself to be used while trying to be useful - I changed that.

I once looked in the mirror and saw someone that was less than, someone not capable, someone that cried because of fear - This has been forever changed.

I am strong, capable, useful, inspiring, powerful and FEARLESS. I am a game changer and I hustle. I love who I am today. Who am I? I am a work of art made up of the pain, fear and scars of my past. Without them I would not know who I really am at this very moment. I am an unstoppable CHAMPION CHANGE MAKER.

Where am I…

I'm around the corner on the other side of fear

I may be what you need to see, or even *who* you need to hear.

Take a step, just one more… find the *strength* inside **you** -

please keep looking, focus… you see me - *I know you do*.

Make a fist, take a stand, push the limit… look this way -

yep, right here, outside your comfort zone - its a *brand new day*.

YOU are unafraid and YOU are strong -

you have a new story, you have a new song.

There's a game you need to change and a hustle for you to find -

The Change

Believe this, now - and clear your mind.

Did you find me, I think you see…

I'm waving, I'm familiar… could it be?

I have your spirit, I have your face, I have your heart - its in a very safe place.

Ignite that hustle, and take my hand, let's change up the game - and make a stand.

I am your strength, waiting on the other side of fear -

Come on over - its awesome here.

REFERENCES

Boyer, Staci. *Motiv8n'U*. United States. Medallion Press. 2010 pg. 248-250

Chopra, Deepak. *Seven Spiritual Laws of Success*.

Oxford Dictionary. http://www.oxforddictionaries.com/us/ . accessed August 15, 2014

To Contact Staci:

Staci@Motiv8nu.com

www.motiv8nu.com

YOU TUBE - www.motiv8nulive.com

Twitter-@Motiv8nu

IG-@Motiv8nu2

FAN PACE www.facebook.com/Motiv8nuThebook

To purchase Staci's motivational Ebook "I Sneezed & Pi$$ed myself, what now?" on iTunes - https://itunes.apple.com/us/book/i-sneezed-pissed-myself/id666087622?mt=11

To purchase Staci's book Motiv8n'U™ on iTunes - https://itunes.apple.com/us/book/motiv8n-u/id789330885?mt=11

To purchase Staci's book Motiv8n'U™ on Amazon - http://www.amazon.com/s/ref=nb_sb_noss?url=search-alias%3Daps&field-keywords=motiv8nu

Award Winning Published Author of *Motiv8n'U* out through Medallion Press

Motiv8n'U Personal Training & Wellness Coaching - Founder & CEO

Motivational Speaker, Personal Trainer, & Wellness Coach,

Fitness Educator, Group Ex Instructor, Pride Nutrition #BikiniAthlete

TEAM Motiv8nU Elite™ Founder / Head Coach

A Pride Affiliate Competition Team

Co-Host of Motiv8nU 360°™

#Motiv8nU4Real

www.Motiv8nU.com

www.StaciBoyer.com

www.TeamMotiv8nu.com

Staci@Motiv8nU.com

Staci@StaciBoyer.com

Cell: 773-351-4646

Your Destiny is NOT by Chance - it is by CHOICE!

Pick up your copy of Motiv8n'U at Barnes & Noble, Amazon.com, Kindle and Ibooks!

LUCAS ROBAK

Lucas J. Robak is a behavior modification coach, , NLP practitioner, speaker, trainer, workshop leader, and author for Skillset Life Coaching. He is also the founder and president of a nonprofit, Melody of Life Foundation.

As a coach and NLP practitioner, Lucas helps his clients replace bad habits with new empowering behaviors. He mainly works with busting limiting beliefs and quitting smoking. Lucas is an inspirational speaker on the power of the mind. He trains and leads workshops on positive thinking, communication, language, purpose/passion, time management and organization.

After being diagnosed with Multiple Sclerosis (MS) on May 29, 2014, Lucas changed the mission of his nonprofit to helping individuals pay for treatment not covered by insurance.

His purpose in life is to bring motivation and inspiration to the world to help them find their passions and live their true definite purpose. One of his passions is to be the person he wishes he had growing up in terms of personal development.

After graduating from college, he soon realized that school does not prepare you for the real world. His mission is to prepare all those who want to improve their lives on a daily basis.

ONLY GOOD CAN COME FROM THIS

By Lucas Robak

"There are two primary choices in life: to accept conditions as they exist, or accept the responsibility for changing them." - Dr. Denis Waitley

Throughout life, there will be events and circumstances that do not fall in your favor. You may have planned for something to happen, and in the end, the outcome that you receive is the complete opposite of what you were searching for. In many situations you could feel like a failure and develop a memory with bad emotions about the event.

There will be other times when something out of your control happens and it changes your life forever, whether that is good or bad. You may have already experienced a sudden death of a loved one, loss of your material possessions or home, losing a job or a natural disaster occurs and does all of the aforementioned.

It does not matter which one of these has happened, the chances of someone telling you, "it will get better with time" or "think positive" is highly likely. We as a society, and individuals, do not know what to say or how to handle situations like these; common phrases seem to be the appropriate response.

As time moves on, you will become busy with life and all the other priorities and obligations that come with it. You become distracted and eventually begin thinking less about what happened to you each day. With this process, it takes a long time before "time" comes around to fix everything.

When people say, "think positive," they're giving the desired end result of where your thoughts should ideally lie. They do not give advice on how to think positive except for the obvious, "just think positive." There is no how to start or where to begin, only the desired state in which we all strive for.

When you look at two individuals from a birds-eye view, they are two similar beings. Both are people with the same features in which humans should have. These individuals are identical in every way in terms of their physical features, but one is poor and happy while the other is wealthy and miserable. What separates them from each other, and us, are our thoughts, our self talk.

The thoughts that we have inside our minds is the only thing that separates us as individuals. The thoughts of these two individuals is what makes the poor individual happy and the wealthy person miserable. All the emotions and perceptions we have come from our thoughts.

> "If you look at what you have in life, you'll always have more. If you look at what you don't have in life, you'll never have enough."
> - Oprah Winfrey

Our thoughts are so vital to our success that this can not be overlooked. The thoughts we have on a daily basis are a direct link to our subconscious; our subconscious controls our emotions and actions. The wealthy have thoughts of delayed income and result producing actions while the poor have thoughts of instant gratification and trading time for dollars. Happy people have thoughts of satisfaction and love while the unhappy individuals have thoughts of fear and being unsatisfied.

Your thoughts will dictate what you do, how you do it, and how you feel both during and after the process. When you are constantly thinking thoughts of love or thoughts of fear, they end up being accepted by your subconscious and start manifesting themselves into your reality. You begin seeing everything you expect to see, whether it is positive or negative. Your thoughts produce world in which only you live in.

> "Change your thoughts and you change your world." - Norman Vincent Peale

What happens when you cannot keep the thoughts of fear and limiting beliefs out of your mind? You know that positive thinking is the best option but you are unable to keep the negative thinking out. How can any good come from this?

When we have thoughts, positive and negative, there are certain neurons in our brains that fire off to each other. Think of it like this: the neurons are friends who extend out their hands and connect for a handshake. We as people are more prone to talk to others who we are comfortable with than strangers we know nothing about. The same concept is happening with the neurons in our brain.

When you are thinking negatively, there is a whole community of neurons communicating with each other and they are loving every minute of it. They are use to it and expect it to happen. Since these "negative thinking neurons" are use to connecting with each other, it is easier for it to happen.

As you catch yourself thinking thoughts you do not want, repeat the word "CANCEL" in your mind until you are able to produce a positive thought and let it flow. You may also do self talk in your mind by telling yourself "these are not the thoughts I want, I am positive and thoughts of love flourish." Get creative here if you would like. The concept is that you are interrupting the negative thoughts and replacing them with empowering, positive images.

When you interrupt your negative thoughts and replace them with positivity, you are stopping the relationship between all the neurons that were firing off to each other and starting up a whole new relationship with the neurons that fire off when you think positively. In time, the relationship between the "negative thinking neurons" will dwindle and the relationship between the "positive thinking neurons" will intensify. As the positive relationship grows stronger, they will expect to fire off on a daily basis and thoughts of abundance, success and love will flourish.

> "Things turn out for the best for those who make the best of how things work out." - John Wooden

Throughout life, we will encounter situations that we did not plan for, nor would we wish upon anyone else to endure. These circumstances could be crimes committed on you or a loved one, a loss of a loved one, not getting into the school of your dreams, not getting the job you were planning on, being diagnosed with a life altering illness, etc. Negative situations happen to everyone in life; what matters is how we look at these negative events. When you look back on the worst thing that has happened to you, how did your life improve because of it?

On May 29, 2014, I was diagnosed with Multiple Sclerosis (MS), which is an autoimmune disease that attacks the nervous system. Imagine if only people's nervous systems were to walk around, we would still be able to tell who is who because the nervous system runs throughout our entire body - internal and external. Now imagine that all the nerves in your body are electrical extension cords. MS gets the immune system to attack the nerves and begins breaking down the insulation (myelin) around them.

Out of the 3 million people that have MS, no two people are the same. This is not a cookie-cutter disease where the same thing happens to everyone. What works for one person could cripple the next. Diet, vitamins, minerals, exercise, acupuncture, massages, mindfulness, positive thinking, meditation, and medication are recommended every day for those with MS. All this information came from decades of statistics on how to successfully live with MS.

Months before I was diagnosed, I began making headway into becoming an author, speaker, trainer and life coach. Everything I did revolved around my life purpose and living with a positive mindset. I was working hard every day to create opportunities and make things happen - for months. Then one day it was becoming more and more difficult for me to walk. After almost two weeks of struggling with my balance, walking, and not being able to hold things in my left hand, I went to the hospital to receive the good news.

The next morning a team of neurologists came in my room to give me my diagnosis. While they were still talking to me, I knew what I had to do with this new "career" that was handed to me. While I was still in the hospital, I began visualizing all the possibilities that can come from me living with MS.

Since my diagnosis, I have been told by countless of people that if anyone should be diagnosed with MS, it is me. My positive attitude and outlook on life drew people closer to me and created better relationships. The nurses told to me many times how they love coming in my room because of the positive energy and how much they laughed. None of this ever would have happened if I was devastated by the news and starting my own little pity party.

> "Challenges are what makes life interesting and overcoming them is what makes life meaningful." - Joshua J. Marine

We are all exactly where we need to be in life. This applies to every second of every day. We are drawn to certain people and events for a particular reason. It is not up to us to figure out the reason at that time. It is up to us to make the best decision that we know we can make. Challenges will arise, and when they do, your decisions and actions will be what creates the future.

When you know that only good will come from all your challenges, you will have more positive thoughts that allow you to make the best decisions possible. With every decision that you make, it takes your life in a different direction than if you would have made the other choice. Keep your "positive thinking neurons" in an active relationship and you will see the best in the toughest difficulties a lot faster and easier.

There may be occasions where you do not see how anything positive could come about what is happening to you right now. That is ok! It is natural for you to only see what is happening according to your perception of the matter. Know that your perception of reality is false 100% of the time. How you perceive an event will be different than how I would perceive that same event.

Perception comes from our conscious minds naturally deleting, distorting and generalizing the information that we receive in life. After all the information we receive on a second-to-second basis will go through these three filters, we have our perception of what we believe to be reality. This can be easily seen in police investigations where they have ten different witnesses to a crime with ten different stories of what happened. These witnesses are not lying either, they truly believe that their perception of the crime is what really happened.

There is so much information that bombards our five senses every second that we naturally delete information that we believe to be irrelevant to us. You may have never seen the car you currently drive on the road until you bought it, now you see them everywhere. That car was always on the road. Your conscious mind was simply deleting that information because it did not pertain to you at the time. This same concept is applied to all areas of your life.

Sometimes we see things for what they are not, we see them for what we want to see. This filter is called distortion. There is an old story about an Indian village who had a deadly snake slithering around causing chaos. One day a villager was walking on a path and saw the snake. He ran back to the village telling everyone about it and getting them into a frenzy. It turned out that it was not a snake, it was a rope. We see what we want to see by distorting the information of the real reality. You will always find what is dominating your thoughts.

The third filter is generalizing. This is when we take our past experiences and knowledge to use it for making sense of the present moment. Someone who had great relationships will see love in every couple they encounter, even when they are fighting. The person who had their heart broken will see a fighting couple and assume it is going to end badly. Each of these individuals will have a different perception of the same couple that is fighting because of their past.

By understanding that your perception is false from reality, you can change your thoughts to change your life. Even if you have one perception about something, it can change through the *Power Behind Positive Thinking*.

"The pessimist sees difficulty in every opportunity. The optimist sees the opportunity in every difficulty." - Winston Churchill

Start developing the thoughts of an optimist to allow yourself to instantly see the good in every difficulty. Challenges are life's gifts to us which helps us grow as individuals. Think of every situation we encounter as training for something bigger and better. Pilots, military, corporate employees, managers, etc., all train to become better at what they do and to be prepared for when challenges arise. By training your mind to be an optimist, you will be empowered when life hands you a challenge.

To get you on the right track of thinking, start noticing the words that you use in your self-talk and with others. As you have thoughts, whether they are positive or negative, they not only create that neuron relationship, they make their way into your subconscious to begin manifesting what you perceive to be true. When you tell people you are broke, you will subconsciously find support to back up that belief. When you tell people you are a smart investor, you will subconsciously start noticing investment opportunities.

You are what you think you are. If you think you are a success, you will see successful results. If you perceive yourself to be a failure, you will see yourself fail. This can happen to someone in all the exact same situations. No matter what happens to you, your thoughts will determine how you perceive the outcome you produce.

To see good in every situation, look at everything as an opportunity. When a problem shows up, do not tell yourself or others that this is a problem, say "we now have a new opportunity." As challenges come in your path, see them as an opportunity to learn and grow. When difficulties arise, look at them as an opportunity to get creative and think critically. All your problems, challenges, and difficulties are stepping stones to your success.

"An obstacle is often a stepping stone." - Prescott

In Jack Canfield's book *The Success Principles*, he details a very empowering formula called E+R=O. This stands for Events + Response = Outcomes. This is a great formula because it gets you to realize that everything you have in life came about because of your thinking and actions. No one created the life that you are living except for you.

Events (E) are the problems, challenges, difficulties, lucky encounters, etc. that are out of our control. These events happen to us whether we like them or not. No matter how much you try to avoid a certain event from happening, this particular event may happen anyway.

Your Response (R) to these events is dictated by your thoughts. The thoughts that you constantly have are what produces the actions other people see. When you control your thoughts and see things from a different perspective, your responses to these events will determine the results you receive.

The Outcome (O) is a direct result from your response to any given event. If you see every situation as an opportunity, you will produce opportunities. If you see every circumstance as a problem, your actions will result with more problems.

When I was diagnosed with Multiple Sclerosis (E), I saw it as an opportunity for me to help those living with MS through motivational speaking on positive thinking. I began contacting numerous people in various organizations through emails and phone calls (R). With a lot of persistence and four months later, I am starting to schedule meetings with people who will be hiring me as a speaker and a Behavior Modification Coach (O). If the same event happened and my response was different, the outcome that I would be living today would be quite different. You choose every outcome that you receive, starting with your thoughts.

> "I am not a product of my circumstances. I am a product of my decisions." - Stephen Covey

There is no situation or circumstance that will stop me from achieving what I set out to achieve. The same goes for you! Everything that is unplanned which comes into your life happens for a reason. These perceived challenges, difficulties, and problems are gifts to train you for what is yet to come.

Look back on all your situations. They are all interconnected which are what turned you into the person that you are today. You are, and will always be, in the perfect place at the perfect time, every second of every day. You would not be where you are now if one little event of your past never happened. It needed to be there in order to make you into who you are now. Control your thoughts and know that only good can come from all situations.

> "The only person you are destined to become is the person you decide to be." - Ralph Waldo Emerson

Contact Info:

Skillset Life Coaching LLC

P.O. Box 210923

Milwaukee, WI 53221

Contact@LucasRobak.com

www.LucasRobak.com

STEPHEN HULTQUIST

Steve Hultquist is considered by many to be one of the foremost business leadership executive coaches in the United States. He advises executive leaders and their teams in widely diverse organizations from the largest Fortune 50 corporations to small early-stage companies and solo entrepreneurs. He works with leaders to create empowering organizations that deliver high value to customers, team members, and suppliers, together with investors and other stakeholders.

Steve knows that ultimately and always, success and profits are about people. His career and leadership includes senior roles in corporate strategy, engineering, professional services, and customer support. His expertise in communication helps organizations identify the benefits to all stakeholders and articulate them with clarity, leading to improved business results - and happier customers and staff.

Steve transforms organizations, aligning motivations across teams and guiding individuals in growing personally and professionally while ensuring that the organization benefits from their growth.

Mr. Hultquist has traveled worldwide as an author and journalist, speaking on topics including delivering value, humanizing business, effective use of technology, organizational leadership, personal development, and human relationships. He has held a wide range of roles including CEO, CTO, CIO, and Chief Evangelist, to deliver exceptionally valuable products and services internationally.

IT'S ALL ABOUT PEOPLE

Business in the Age of Relationships

By Stephen Hultquist

The customer isn't always right.

I remember walking into the newly finished executive center at the IBM facility in Boulder, Colorado. The high-tech windows used LED shutters, and when they were activated, the glass cleared to allow visitors to observe the state-of-the-art customer support center below. Customer support specialists took phone calls, and statistics tracked their activities. It was extremely impressive, and it sold many large contracts. It was also all wrong.

For more than twenty years, the most influential businesses have focused their customer support efforts on tracking the activities of their staff, telling them what to do, making sure they do it quickly, correcting them when they don't, and firing them if they don't change. It's been a churn-and-burn cycle that has seen customer service continue on a downward spiral.

Why? Because the focus is all wrong.

The industrial age led business managers to believe that measurement, metrics, and modification was the best path to profit and success. We see it today on Wall Street with short-term perspectives and the weak economic consequences of this thinking.

Smart business leaders will see this and change.

From Friends to the World

In July, 2014, Duff Watson of New Hope, Minnesota was removed from a Southwest Airlines airplane because he posted to Twitter that a gate agent treated him rudely. After being seated on the plane, he said he tweeted, "RUDEST AGENT IN DENVER. KIMBERLY S. GATE C39. NOT HAPPY @SWA" and shortly thereafter was removed from the plane, told to delete his tweet if he wanted to fly because the gate agent felt threatened; and after doing so, he and his family were allowed back on the plane.

For a usually smart company with employees known for their senses of humor, this was a real surprise. There is no way to know what really happened, and the various on-line conversations about this incident run the gamut of possible responses. Regardless of what happened, though, the situation underscores the truth that the world has changed. Ubiquitous Internet and social media connections are creating frictionless communication for everyone.

How will you handle this?

There was a time when a disgruntled customer would tell his friends. Today, he tells the world.

Although it's a common and trite saying, the customer isn't always right. However, it's critical for everyone in the organization to treat them like they are.

In the case of the Southwest Airlines gate agent, it is likely that she is measured on her activities, such as how quickly she boards the plane and whether or not they close the door on time. This leads to the kind of interactions anyone who has flown anywhere sees: rushed and frazzled travelers interacting with frustrated and distracted employees. There is likely plenty of blame to go around. However, the response of Southwest's corporate communications was also surprisingly lacking. Typically, they respond with humor and in a way that communicates the value they place on both their customers and their employees. They acknowledged the incident and said only, "The incident is currently under review." Oops.

This new era makes responding well more difficult. You won't be "right" all the time. You can't measure how well you interact with customers and put the metrics on a spreadsheet and display it on a high-tech flat screen. You have to engage with fellow human beings and figure it out.

This era is about relationships. In a back-to-the-future kind of way, technology has brought us so far that we are now once again interacting as individuals and not as groups. Gone are the easy labels and simple equations telling us that a customer support call should last less than 5.97 minutes. Gone are the days of monitoring employees, sending surveys, and scripting customer service. Industry has responded with ideas like Customer Engagement which the Advertising Research Foundation defined as, "...turning on a prospect to a brand idea enhanced by the surrounding context."

It's actually much simpler than that. And much riskier.

Surprise of surprises, it's all about people.

From Numbers to People

From the second half of the 19th century through the first half of the 20th, the modern world was born through industry and technology. In the United States and other major economic powers, there was a massive shift from a widespread agrarian populace to one concentrated in urban areas to serve as the masters of machines that were the engine of economics. In the process, entire approaches to education and maturation were turned over wholesale to methods that would support the requirements of a manufacturing industrial economy: rule following, procedural, hierarchical organizations ruled by those with the capital to own the means of production.

This social structure is a relatively recent invention that served a specific need, but, it is rapidly losing its reason for existence. Those old industrial roles are being more often performed by robotics and computer-controlled systems, meaning there are fewer people needed to get the work done. The new revolution swings the pendulum back from nameless, faceless humans doing repetitive work to people as individuals interacting with one another based on who they are, what they can do for one another, and how well they can do it. It's all about people.

How does this impact your business and career?

It is easy to forget the fundamental truth underneath all business activity: people make decisions. People make decisions to buy or not to buy a product or service. They decide how much is too much, and when it's worth it. Ultimately, whether it's a small personal purchase or a multi-billion dollar acquisition, people make decisions. So, knowing how people make choices will help you whether you are responsible for making the decision or working to have someone decide in your favor.

Decisions

Those involved in the process make decisions for many reasons, some conscious and some unconscious. Ultimately, they choose based on what they believe will help them to change their lives for the better or to avoid some negative situation that they fear. Once you begin looking at the choices you face personally and the decisions those impacting your business make in the same way, the smoke clears. You begin to see what is really going on behind the mystery. As a result, you can begin to communicate in a way that resonates and helps your customer make the best choice for you and for them.

Research shows us that everyone makes decisions based on their emotional response to the situation. After we make a decision, we gather logical rationale to support it. However, we make the decision based on our emotional response to the choice we face.

Participating in a market means offering products and services that prospects see as providing a path to what they desire. Some people desire experiences. For others, it's essential to fulfill obligations, responsibilities, and our relationships to others. Respect and status are primary motivations for some. Others seek unique and impacting experiences. Interestingly, different generations focus on different outcomes, with experiences becoming a higher priority than traditional goals such as owning a home or a nice car for the emerging generation.

As we take on different roles, they also change our priorities; moving our motivations around and triggering emotions differently. Consider, too, how phases of life result in alternative emphasis, such as being single, being in a relationship, being married, having children, being divorced, or becoming empty-nesters. Each of these phases will influence how a choice activates our emotions.

Learn how to understand your customers and their emotional responses based on their lives and priorities. As a result, you can communicate in a way that will make it easy for them to decide in your favor.

How do you learn to understand? This is the tough one: you get to know them. Every interaction with another person is part of a relationship. It may be brief, like the conversation at the counter when you buy a cup of coffee, or it may be very involved over a long project or negotiation. It's still a relationship; and when you approach it as one human being working through what's important to the parties involved in the relationship, you dramatically increase your potential for success. It starts with getting to know them.

A few months ago, I was on the phone with a friend who had a job as an inside sales rep for a technology company. She was telling me about her frustration in setting up a call with an executive with a large city government, only to have the sales call with the outside sales rep go poorly. "They didn't even ask any questions!" she complained. I asked her who she meant by "they," and she said, "The customer. And I know we could really help them." That's when I gave her the bad news: it's not the job of the prospect to ask questions. It's the job of the salesperson. That's the first step in getting to know your prospect to find out whether or not you can help them: you ask questions. The second step happens at the same time:

you listen carefully to the answers they give and keep asking questions to understand better and better their needs and wants.

Of course, this takes work. It also helps if you actually care about what they need and want. Isn't that the starting point for all great relationships? What it takes is to focus first on the other person, or as Dr. Stephen Covey put it in his seminal book *The Seven Habits of Highly Effective People,* "Seek first to understand, then to be understood."

I remember a gray spring afternoon a few years ago when the clouds were building over the Rockies as I reluctantly reached for the phone in the kitchen. The ominous weather reflected my mood as I prepared to call and cancel my TV service. I didn't want to deal with the counter-offers, grilling, and delaying tactics that I knew would come. I growled to myself, but called, anyway. It was going to be a long afternoon. The customer support representative did not want to believe that I needed to cancel. He insisted on knowing why I wanted to cancel. He sent me to a second level of support. They insisted on having a follow-up call after I finished. And more. While I was able to get the cancellation completed, it was painful and took far longer than it should have. Believe it or not, I still receive mail from them offering me all kinds of incentives to return as a customer. I will say this: nothing that they have done in this process would make me likely to return as a customer.

What makes them think that it would? Someone at that company obviously believes that they can convince me to return by offering me various "deals" to convince me that I will pay less for TV service. You may wonder what the problem is with that. Simple: My reasons for leaving have nothing to do with TV service or cost. Until they figure that out, there is nothing that they can say or do that will change my decision. At this point, they've sent me so much irrelevant mail that I simply toss it all into the recycle bin without even opening it. They are spending money on useless efforts.

I travel worldwide to work with organizations based on their needs and desires. As a result, I set up my cellular service to have international services and then take them off when I am in the States for a while. After one of my last trips, I checked my project list as I sat down in my office. It had been a full week since I returned to Colorado from India when it struck me that I hadn't cancelled my international cellular plan. Ugh! Now I'd have to call my cellular company and deal with the morass of options. Reluctantly, I called. I was greeted by a cheerful voice. In just a few minutes, she had not only removed the service, but had asked questions, determined the best, most cost effective approach, explained to me the options and her recommendations, and made sure I had received what I wanted. What a difference!

Clearly, cellular carriers and TV service providers are among the most notorious in all of customer service. However, I had opposite experiences. The biggest difference from my perspective was an effort to understand my needs and wants, ask questions, comprehend the answers, and then let me know how their organization could address my needs.

The key is to know what questions to ask and how to respond to the answers. Do you know the key concerns of your primary customers and how you can address them? Your primary customer may be your boss, another member of your organization, or a customer or prospect for your company's product or service, but whoever he or she is, your customer has needs and wants for you to address. How will you find them?

Motivation

As you look hard at your approach to understanding others, it helps to understand motivation. As an executive leadership coach, I help executives understand that it isn't possible for them to motivate their teams. That's not how motivation works. Let's step back and consider what motivation is. It is the drive from within that moves a person from desire to action. While psychology suggests that there are both intrinsic and extrinsic drives, the important insight for relationships is that motivation comes from within. Any extrinsic motivation works only insomuch as it addresses an internal drive. For example, paying a bonus or threatening firing works only because the person values something deeper that requires that money or keeping the job. However, you know situations where the bonus wasn't enough, the options for other positions were too great, or there were other reasons that the promises or threats were insufficient motivation.

This is important to consider as you ask your questions and seek to understand the motivation of your customer. What really matters to them? Perhaps they want to impress their boss. Perhaps they have a child going into college. Perhaps they are looking for industry recognition. Whatever it is, there are hidden intrinsic motivations that your questions can uncover and provide you with the underlying reasons for the choices that she will make. Ask questions. Care about her as a person. Frame your solution in those terms. If you don't have a solution for what matters most, be clear and honest about it and earn the right to help solve problems and address needs in the future.

Benefits or Features

Alpine skiing is one of the passions of my life. I have had the blessing of skiing all over the US and even had an incredible trip to the Alps a few years ago. One way to talk about a ski resort is to lay out its numbers: for example, my home resort of Copper Mountain has over 140 trails, 23 lifts, 2465 acres of skiable terrain, 12,313 summit, 9,712 base, 2,601 feet vertical drop, 23 chair-lifts, 32,324 skiers per hour lift capacity.

Sound exciting?

Not really. What I can tell you, though, is that if you come ski with me at Copper, you'll have one of the most incredible experiences of your life. You can ski any terrain you enjoy, from the easiest greens isolated from the speeding masses, to steep, rugged terrain accessible only by snow cat or hiking that offers fresh tracks in the "steep and deep." You will experience the amazing sensation of magic snow; the Colorado fluff that is soft and easy to ski. I will even share with you some of the secret stashes that hold snow for a day or two after a storm, so you can experience the ultimate in Colorado skiing. Now do you want to come play in the snow with me?

If you're a skier, you will, because now you know why you should come and visit.

One of the most common mistakes I see with communications even once someone recognizes that they need to focus on the relationship is that they then emphasize the features of the product or service. Talking about what the product will do, how it does it, the numbers that show how much better it is all seem logical. Why shouldn't you tell a prospect all about the offer so they can recognize all of the valuable capabilities? Simple: ultimately, the features are about you and your product.

Instead, talk about whatever matters to the people on the other side of the conversation. You've asked questions to understand what matters to them, now help them imagine how much better their situation will be once they are working with you. Tell them clearly and emotionally. Make it easy for them to make their decision. Always check your language and make sure you are talking about them and their concerns, not yourself and your offerings. If you really care about them, too, it'll show.

Making the Change

So, how do you make the change?

This morning I sat across a small table at a local Boulder coffee shop challenging a 66 year old man to step into his own life and make his own choices. To recognize that his life to this point is the summation of the thoughts he has had and choices he has made, and the rest of his life will be a result of how he thinks and chooses from here to the end. He had tears in his eyes as he recognized his responsibility to himself and his culpability in how his life has evolved to this point.

The good news is that he can change it NOW!

And so can you.

The key question is, will you?

To Contact Steve:

Steve "ssh" Hultquist can be reached at ssh@infinitesummit.com (303) 731-6877, and http://infinitesummit.com

The Change

SALLY HOLMES REED

Ever feel like you have what it takes, but something always seems to get in the way? Or do you know what is holding you back, but you haven't been able to find your way to success? Sally Holmes Reed is considered by many to be one of Seattle's best Hypnotherapists, helping business leaders like you break through to new levels of success. Sally is the founder of <u>ChannelYourSuccess.com</u> and creator of the Channel Your Success Formula. As an Author, Master NLP Hypnotherapist, Transformational Results Coach, and Energy Healer, Sally has helped thousands of clients clear their fears, overcome obstacles, and challenge their limitations so they can step into bigger opportunities in their life and business. Sally's mission is to help people lead fulfilling lives and experience extraordinary success.

CHANNEL YOUR SUCCESS

By Sally Holmes Reed

This is your life. It belongs to you. Would you like your future self to be living a happy, healthy, active, prosperous life, full of love and laughter, in a whole new way? What if you start where you are right now and begin to move in a new direction towards what you want to create in your life? The smallest course correction will be enough for you to end up in a whole new and better place.

Whether you want to lose your old lousy life or make your great life even better, when you begin to channel your success you will leave behind whatever has been holding you back from having a life that is better than you ever expected.

So as you join me on this unique personal transformational activation, you will take a journey unlike anything you have ever experienced before, to claim your healthier, happier, abundant, new future self filled with love and appreciation and gratitude for all the blessings life has to offer.

This activation will allow you to begin to channel your success as you access the creative part of yourself at higher levels of expanded consciousness, where change can take place in an easy and effortless way. Wouldn't you like to move out of all your past limitations and hidden conflicts that have been keeping you from having what you want, so you can step into a bright new future that supports you completely in making positive changes in your life, starting right now?

Remember, this is about your empowerment, your transformation, your success, so don't be surprised when you begin to see yourself in a whole new light.

Stop now and take a breath. Not just any breath. A breath that calls in your life force energy, your living light stream of love. Tune into your own unique Soul Frequency, which illuminates the highest and best version of yourself. Expand your mind as you connect with all that the universe has to give. Bring this new expansive energy and vitality to your mind and body and life. Feel the magic of discovering and following your own inner path to enlightenment, raising your vibration higher and higher. Channeling your own wellspring of love and light and life.

Keep breathing all the way down into the center of yourself. On your next breath make a gentle HAAAAAA sound as you follow that breath all the way out... letting the sound of your breathing begin to resonate with every cell of your body, as you begin to tune into your whole body more and more efficiently.

What if you can breathe in all the love and goodness you need, allowing it to fill you completely? Then imagine it overflowing out to your entire life.

Notice how you are now able to begin to experience this deep state of relaxation, becoming more and more comfortable, as your mind becomes calmer and clearer with every breath you take... letting all the pieces fall into place in an easy and effortless way.

What if you can begin to simply let go of any attachments to anyone or anything, to any where or any when, while allowing everything unimportant to simply fade away, dissolving and disappearing completely?

So from now on, with every breath you take, imagine breathing in all that you need... letting your body expand and receive, as you fill yourself completely. Imagine breathing in love and appreciation and gratitude into every cell of your body, right into the heart of your own DNA, which will allow you to begin releasing whatever needs to be released on all levels of consciousness.

Now imagine, with every breath you take, you can release all that you no longer want or need. Breathing out any negative memories, thoughts or feelings; any doubt or worry or fear; any hesitation or resistance. Breathing out anything you may have been carrying around up until now; any shame or blame or pain; any grudges or regret; any unforgiveness, helplessness or hopelessness... breathing out all that does not support you completely in creating success in your life.

No longer be afraid to step out of the old and into the light, free from the way it has always been.

It may feel as if you can now begin to reach for the stars... beginning to harmonize with the new frequencies that are coming to you now and causing a wave of reorganization on all levels of consciousness, as you naturally adjust to what is most comfortable for your mind and body and life.

Allow yourself to enter your imagination and find that comfortable, peaceful, place within you, where you can be exactly who you want to be... creating this new space within for you to begin to receive whatever it is you are wanting to receive, as quickly as that.

And as you continue inhaling slowly and deeply, once again breathing in and filling yourself all the way up to your collar bone... holding for just a moment as you activate the relaxation response in the center of your brain and allowing this fresh oxygen to wash through every cell of your body, from the top of your head, to the tips of your fingers, to the soles of your feet...

This time, as you exhale, simply open your mind, release your thoughts and connect with your heart, so you can continue to tune into your body more and more efficiently. Because now your inner mind will continue working all by itself to open you up to the truth within... allowing you to change your way of life right to the core, as you let your true self shine through, becoming brighter and brighter and brighter.

What if you can return to this healthy, relaxed state, over and over again, as you to continue to feel better in every way?

Breathe in unconditional love and life and light.

Breathe out any disbelief, any doubt or worry or fear, any tension, holding or resistance. Release all obstacles… simply letting go completely of whatever is preventing you from reaching your dreams.

And now with every breath you take, you will begin to notice that you are becoming more and more comfortable with this new process of change, because change always happens. As you activate this new flow of change, you will begin to take inspired action as you move toward fulfilling your dreams and enjoying every step along the way.

What if you can simply allow your expanded consciousness to take over? Because your expanded consciousness knows exactly what to do and is doing it, right now, in just the right way. Take all the time you need and just allow it to happen naturally, without having to think about it at all, as you easily and effortlessly continue to release the past and reset those old dysfunctional default settings. Neutralize and eliminate any interference… uniting all parts of yourself into wholeness and completion. Step into your new future that now supports you completely.

So from now on, today and every day, as you step into your new future that is light and joyful, whenever you feel any stress in your life; any of the doubt or worry or fear that you used to have before now; any untrue, critical, or judgmental thoughts; any anxieties; anything you may feel uncertain about; or anything that is holding you back from having a life that is better than you ever imagined, then here is what you can do:

Simply stop as you bring your full awareness into the present moment and take a nice deep breath into the center of yourself, into your heart. With that breath, begin to breathe in all the love and goodness you need and have been asking for. Bring it all in now.

Allow this wonderful sense of well-being to wash through every cell of your body, filling you with compassion and insight. Sense it easily moving up through your whole body and then overflowing from the top of your head, to the tips of your fingers, to the soles of your feet, restoring all to balance and harmony on all levels of consciousness. Just let that continue automatically in whatever way works best for you and your whole body.

Now let's send your awareness down to the soles of your feet for just a moment. What if you can pretend that you can imagine that you have magnets on the soles of your feet that can connect you into the Earth's magnetic crystalline grid? Perhaps you begin to feel fully grounded and supported by the Earth below you while allowing your energy to be cleansed and renewed by this connection.

Now, imagine that you can pretend to send your awareness deep into the center of the Earth... perhaps discovering a beautiful, gigantic, iron core crystal in the center of the Earth that is generating life force energy just for you. Imagine that you can safely and securely ground into the crystalline core of the Earth and begin to deeply draw on all the energy you discover there.

Feel that crystalline Earth core energy traveling back up and entering through the soles of your feet, then easily moving up through your legs, and through your lower back. As this energy continues traveling up, opening and activating all of your energy centers, sense that it can begin spinning your new life into motion, in tune with the rhythms of Nature. Just like the Earth revolves around our Sun and our solar system revolves around the Galactic Core, this energy can spiral up through your entire belly and solar plexus, then through your lungs and heart, moving up through your throat, through the base of your neck and into all parts of your brain, filling your whole head completely.

Take a moment to imagine every cell of your body completely filled with this crystalline light new Earth energy... opening easily and effortlessly to receive on all levels of consciousness, and letting that continue in whatever way works best for you and your whole body.

Now if you send your awareness to the top of your head for just a moment, pretend that you can you imagine that you can expand your consciousness out through the top of your head and up through all dimensions.

Imagine this expanded consciousness is able to continue spiraling up, moving up and out of space and time, and leaving the old behind. Feel yourself peeling off and unraveling, layer after layer. As you imagine yourself doing this, you uplift the frequency of your vibration, letting in more and more light. As you reach higher and higher, it seems as if the Universe has opened its doors just for you, allowing you to move through the gateway to all understanding. When you cross this threshold, your reality will be transformed, as you step into the light of infinite possibilities.

With every step you take, you now are able to reach higher and higher until you discover a beautiful golden white crystalline light, filled with all the colors of the rainbow. You notice this light from Source has a pulsing radiance and is brighter than all the light you have ever seen. You can see that it is showering down from the quantum field of All That Is, where all is light. This is a divine radiance from the Great Central Sun at the center of the Universe, humming with the sacred elemental sound waves of the ancient melody of Om. Om is the sound of creation. Begin experiencing these light waves of grace, in harmonic resonance, perhaps beyond all understanding, as you tune in on all levels of consciousness.

Let's imagine, as you step into this light from Source, that you experience a wonderful feeling of melting in, and blending in, washing over you as you merge into what seems like shimmering golden liquid light. Somehow you know that this golden light can transform you, as if you can departiculate into the Oneness of All That Is.

Feel this golden liquid light dissolving away any heaviness, any density, any attempts to control, any old programming, any imprints or blocks, any attachment to cause and effect, any old victim or survival consciousness, any opposing force, as well as melting away any beliefs that may interfere with your total success.

No longer do you ever have to be empowered by struggle, as this golden light continues neutralizing anything that does not support you. Clear away anywhere you were wounded or weakened, any place you were fragmented or disconnected, any time your power has been lost or stolen. Allow all that to simply dissolve away and disappear completely.

By collapsing all time into oneness - past, present, and future - you can begin restoring all to balance, harmony and perfection.

Continue letting go and allowing all to be resolved and dissolved. You may begin to feel lighter and lighter and lighter, so let that continue in whatever way works best for you and your whole body.

With a knowing that now you are in tune with the energy of creation, begin to open up to all aspects of who you are. Stay connected to your higher, wiser self, an expanded being of light, reuniting your entire energy body on all levels of consciousness. Through this process you are activating your Divine Multi-Dimensional You, your Light Body that exists in your unique soul frequency within the oneness of Unity Consciousness, forever tuning into your Soul Source connection.

And as you stand in that stream of your living golden white crystalline Love Light, you bond with your highest, infinite, Divine Soul Self, and begin to shine brighter and brighter and brighter. From this new higher perspective, you can easily look into your future and find that place where you have expanded your life to include all that you are now joyfully creating, the life you desire, where all your success is occurring. Within this future hologram you are re-inventing your reality and creating the story of who you will become. Make it a good one.

With this activation you bring together your Self in this moment of now, along with your higher, infinite, Divine Self, and your Future Self into perfect alignment, creating your own personal unity consciousness - what I like to call your Soulistic Self.

Now, follow this stream of golden white crystalline Love Light all the way back to here on Earth, connecting with your Heart, creating a sacred inner sanctuary where your Soulistic Self can now reside. And as you do, all parts of yourself from the past, present, and future are brought together, perhaps for the first time… reclaiming all aspects of who you are… no longer letting any part of you be locked away, stuck in the past, or frozen in time. Integrating all that you are into wholeness and completion, where you move into an even larger realm of expanded conscious awareness and creation, evolving new ways of being on all levels of consciousness.

Now imagine this beautiful stream of golden white crystalline Love Light from Source, permanently showering down on you. Imagine it surrounding you completely. Feel how good it will feel to seal yourself in with this beam of golden white crystalline living light stream of love, perhaps experiencing a sense of personal sovereignty for the first time… allowing you to feel safe and secure in the center of yourself.

And now, what if you can move your whole life into this golden white crystalline light? Illuminate your experiences, your environment, your relationships, your work, and your entire life in this golden white crystalline living light stream of love.

Because now you can feel free to take a deep breath of relief and release and relaxation, restoring a state of grace to your whole mind and body and life, creating balance and harmony in this whole new way. Allow wonderful feelings of freedom, calm, and control to begin to flow freely through your entire mind and body and life. And by doing so, you begin to experience complete emotional wellness, feeling happier than you have ever felt before.

Realizing the power of your full presence and awareness will bring success to all areas of your life. Feel like you have it now, because you can, and you will, and you do allow it to happen automatically, today and every day and on into your new future that supports you completely. When you allow this feeling of wellbeing to wash through every cell of your body, then everything in life begins to work in creatively fulfilling ways.

Begin to notice what is different in your life starting right now as you begin discovering new insights and creative solutions that are now resonating with your highest good. Connecting with your own inner guidance, you can intuitively feel what is real and right in each moment. Recovering the full dimensionality of all that you are, you become a wholly conscious creator and begin to channel your success.

With your new and powerful feelings of comfort, confidence, and wellbeing, you will return to being fully present in your body, while being thoroughly grounded and supported by the Earth below you and connected to your living light stream of love from Source above… feeling centered and peaceful in each moment of now.

What if you can now easily allow new possibilities unlike anything you have experienced before, going beyond what you ever expected? Allow this activation on all levels of consciousness to continue, so you can start to channel your success, have what you want and create the life you desire, starting right now.

To contact Sally:

To Learn more about how to remove blocks and hidden conflicts so you can take the leap to higher levels of success and achievement. Claim your special CHANNEL YOUR SUCCESS training and begin to rise up to the next level in your life and business at www.ChannelYourSuccess.com or ask a question at Sally@HypnosisSeattle.com.

PEGGY CARUSO

Peggy Caruso has 22 years experience, is an 8-time Entrepreneur, the Author of 4 books and has been featured on Word-of-Mom radio and many radio stations across the US. She hosts a talk show, "Ask The Expert" on WCED in DuBois, PA. Peggy has been featured in New Living Magazine and is also a sponsor for Word-of-Mom radio.

In addition to being an Executive and Personal Development Coach, Peggy is an advanced NLP Master Practitioner and Trainer, Hypnotherapist, and certifies individuals to become a Life Coach. Her education allows her to expand her typical life coaching client base to assist those with ADD/ADHD and depression. She assists in getting children and adults off of their depression medication; which benefits them by recognizing their issues and being able to move forward in a positive direction.

Peggy also assists entrepreneurs, executives, stay-at-home moms, college students, teens and children.

REVOLUTIONIZE YOUR FAMILY'S LIFE

By Peggy Caruso

She came into my office in tears and began by telling me her story...

"As I am driving up the driveway to the house there are tears streaming down my face. Coming home from a day at the office, but then realizing, what is home? Having a career as a County Commissioner is very stressful, but has always been rewarding. How does someone feel as though they have a perfect life only to find that it is filled with lies and deception? Is this real? And if so, why me?

I thought my husband and I had a perfect marriage. Sure, we experience the challenges of life, but we've always been able to work through those obstacles with love. I always looked at our relationship as one that consists of great intimacy, laughter, friendship, communication and trust. Today, I realize that it actually consists of dishonesties and a lack of marital value.

She – "the other woman" presented herself to me today, informing me that she is in love with my husband. With an appointed position I am in constant scrutiny with the public. What will I tell people? How and when did this happen? How could I be so blind? I didn't know how to respond. I was sad, angry, and most of all, confused.

After she leaves my office, I sit at my desk in total disheartenment, and then the downward spiral begins. My phone rings and it is the school informing me that my son, who is a senior in high school, was caught with marijuana. My beautiful son – honor student, star of the basketball team, voted most popular and now... drugs?

The only person left is my daughter who I also thought is doing great. Do I need to inquire about her as well? With what I learned about my husband and son, I knew I needed to check on my daughter. I received a wonderful report. I stopped and gave gratitude for at least one blessing in the middle of this mess. She is a sophomore in high school and is doing well thus far. So the question is how do you raise two children the same way and end up with different results?"

She wanted an answer as to how this scenario could happen to her and she wanted to know the underlying cause. The most challenging part of this situation is the unknown. This particular client felt as though she had the perfect family and in minutes she found the complete opposite. Not just one setback, but several. The problems that were just discovered with her husband and son could now have a negative impact on her well-adjusted daughter, due to the stress it will inevitably create in their household. Even though she was doing well right now, what will happen to her and how will all of this situation affect her?

We first determined that she wanted to save the marriage, but we needed to see if her husband was willing to work things out. Fortunately, he did. So they began the coaching process. In deciding to repair what was left of their marriage and rebuild the family, there needed to be forgiveness and calmness of mind. Forgiveness allows the individual to move forward in a positive manner and there can be no solid decision making when there is clutter and confusion in the mind.

What does that mean? Behavioral patterns in people are caused by their actions, which are produced from thoughts and feelings. Your thoughts produce your feelings and your feelings produce your actions, so if you want to change your actions you must begin by changing your thoughts. What that means is whatever is impressed upon the subconscious mind is a direct result of what your conscious mind has accepted.

Your conscious mind is your reasoning mind and has the ability to accept or reject a thought at the conscious level. However, once you accept it, it goes into your subconscious mind and is believed to be true. Your subconscious mind does not reason so it accepts what is impressed – good or bad, positive or negative – it doesn't care.

Let's look at the marital issue first. After extensive questioning it is evident that balancing career and family obligations was a huge issue and the wife couldn't understand that if you don't find that balance you are unable to comprehend problematic areas. The husband, who is an accountant, has a less demanding position than that of a County Commissioner. She would do many evening meetings leaving her husband to attend to family. Communication became lost due to being stressed and tired. Stress is caused from fear, worry, doubt, and indecision.

Her stress also caused irritability, leaving the husband feeling as though he was unable to have a conversation with her relative to family matters. I first worked with both of them on communication skills. Then I introduced skills that could also help them communicate better with their children. I taught them to ask good questions. What happens? One person says something that causes irritation or confusion with the other and they then carry it around with them for days before bringing it to the surface. Upon bringing it out, the argumentative statements begin. Whenever someone experiences lack of communication, confusion or anger, begin by calmly asking questions to assist the other person with understanding feelings. Once you can feel what the other person is feeling, your perception changes.

This is carried over to other family members. The son felt the animosity between the parents and became withdrawn for fear of creating additional stress. This caused him to internalize on his emotions; which can lead to anger issues, cutting, alcohol, narcotics, social issues, etc. In this case, it led to marijuana, which was an escape so he didn't have to deal with stress from family. He had added pressure for fear of failing. He continually worried about his grades and being the best in sports because he did not want to disappoint his family, but I taught him that failure is good. I encourage it. Failure is just feedback letting you know how to modify your plan – stepping stones to success. All of the successful people in history have had multiple failures before reaching success.

His academic performance was great and he had great leadership skills; however, in similar cases, there have been client's who were less fortunate in keeping it all together. Many clients become socially withdrawn as well, causing simultaneous issues such as being bullied or becoming a bully. When a child becomes withdrawn there are many factors that are the underlying cause, such as social media, video games, family stress, etc., and many parents are too busy to notice. This is quite common in today's society when both parents have to manage career and family.

Technology is a difficult subject, but as with anything, you must find the balance. It is a very good tool if used correctly and in moderation. You need to advance with technology, but you must understand that you need to enhance communication skills.

I taught the son and the daughter the importance of success principles and encourage them even in small children. In those principles I help them discover their skill sets and implement goal planning. Once you've established each of those, you can implement other tools and techniques to place them in the entrepreneurial mindset. Teaching them to become a 'Kid-preneur' will help them succeed as adults.

I also implemented masterminding with the teens because of the dying art of communication due to technology. Masterminding is placing a group of like-minded students together to meet an hour every week or bi-weekly. They take turns at each other's home. It assists with reinforcing interpersonal relations, problem solving and accountability. It teaches them the importance of being grateful for their "wins" and assists with overcoming obstacles. The group works together to offer solutions to each challenge and provides trust, sincerity and support.

The daughter implemented a vision board. A vision board is an exercise in which they find pictures in magazines or from the Internet that reflect their goals. Placing it on the screen of their mind is beneficial in making it a reality. Creative imagination is vital to their lives. It is the receiving set of the brain. So use your senses and make it a reality. Making a vision board is a fun exercise for anyone to do with their children. Have them look at it daily and keep it in their rooms so they can see it when they awake and before going to bed. You can also place pictures on their iPad or iPod where they view it often.

Working together to overcome challenges assists them with an attitude of gratitude. Positive affirmations and being grateful for the good things in life places them in a positive energy flow, which will assist them with attracting positive things in their lives.

Assisting the son with the aforementioned success principles helped him with motivation, persistence, and the desire to succeed. So, how were two children raised in the same household with the same principles and have different perceptions and outcomes? That is a question so commonly raised by parents. There are many things that factor into it. For example, understanding the developmental periods of a child's life. The imprint period is from birth to age seven and this is where the parents have the biggest influence on the child. It is what they impress on their child's mind. There is no critical factor in children; which means they have nothing to compare to what is impressed upon their subconscious mind. In other words, if a parent tells a child (in the imprint period) that the sky is purple, the child would believe it because they have nothing to compare with that information.

The modeling period is next and from ages seven to fourteen. This is where the biggest changes take place. They don't just model family, but also friends, TV stars, singers, etc., so the two children can break away on their belief system during this period due to outer influences and different interests. They each had their own set of friends who also had different interests, so even though the parental values were equal, behavioral changes began to take place.

They then move into the socialization period, which is from ages fourteen to twenty-one. This period is where they unconsciously determine what is important. They break away from the modeling period and become individualized by beginning to form their own identity. They are unaware that they are creating their own reality and habits in the subconscious mind, and this can be dangerous. That is why we are still living out our paradigm

– our many behavior patterns that result in habits stored in our subconscious minds since childhood. The habits follow us into adulthood. We choose to follow that behavior because it is our reality and believe it to be true. It is familiarity.

Children who possess strong positive beliefs create a wonderful life and contribute positively to others. This inner belief builds strong self-esteem, which will allow them to navigate through their teenage years with positivity. When children become teenagers they tend to break away from their parents and test the waters. This is part of the socialization period. If they have a strong inner sense they will make positive choices. This will help them avoid the problems of peer pressure, drugs, bullying and other destructive behaviors.

So, how did this information help the family? I coached the parents to promote self-awareness, which is the inner core of their well being. Communication was the most influential factor in creating marital disengagement. Effectively communicating prevents anger and malice. As in many marriages, they began to experience a decline in all the little areas that need continual attention. I began to teach them balance with career and family obligations, focus and family structure. I provided many tools and techniques they could continually utilize to provide the recognition to self-saboteurs, which are obstacles that we create within ourselves.

Understanding the complexities of the subconscious mind and behavioral patterns allowed them to become cognizant of their own personal saboteurs… therefore, assisting them with growth and repair. Forgiveness is a key factor. You must forgive in order to move forward, and it allowed them to recognize the detriment to giving in to negative influences and to safeguard them with preventative measures. They began to apply gratitude, and rekindle many parts of their marriage starting with a date night.

It was a difficult process, but the process began with both of them being able to recognize the obstacles, observe where they came from, and provide tools and techniques to move ahead with love and positivity.

The son had to be able to discover why his behavior changed and what his own saboteurs were as well. We had to rebuild communication and work toward goal setting and success principles. He was involved in a great circle of friends, which proved to be beneficial in working with positives. His academic performance was above average, therefore indicating good self-esteem, persistence, and motivation.

Areas of concern with him were technology issues, so I provided educational material on internet safety. He began to internalize his emotion and spent a lot of time in his room alone, which enhances depression. I worked with him extensively on getting him to recognize and release issues. He experienced worry, fear and doubt, so I gave him multiple exercises he could implement to begin the process of eliminating those negative influences.

I also coached the daughter to ensure she had no underlying issues and assisted her with being able to deal with these family challenges. It is difficult for children to endure a family experience that is extremely negative when their inner belief is that of a "perfect" family. She now had to realize there was a dark side, and implement coping strategies. I also worked on strengthening her subconscious mind.

Balancing career and family life is one of the biggest challenges in American households today. There never seems to be enough time in the day to "do it all." This family was no exception to this issue. And while an affair for the husband and smoking marijuana for the son were detrimental, negative events, with the willingness to make changes and the proper tools and techniques to do so, this family was repaired before irreparable damage was done.

Please feel free to contact Peggy for a FREE 30-minute consultation.

Phone: 814-335-4314

Email: pcaruso@lifecoaching.comcastbiz.net

peg.caruso@lifecoachingandbeyond.com

Website: www.lifecoachingandbeyond.com

Peggy's newest book, *Revolutionize Your Child's Life* - Foreword by Bob Proctor, #1 International Best Selling Author, is now available in Amazon, Barnes & Noble, Kindle and many online book stores.

Book Overview

The world our children are growing up in today is vastly different from the one we recall as we think back to our own adolescence. It is not only the typical changes we see occurring from one generation to the next, but a whole new component to parenting that has been added with the rapid growth of technology. Couple these changes with the dynamics of what constitutes a family, balancing the busy life of career and home, and taking preventative measures to safeguard our children against negativity.

We all want our children to excel and lead happy, productive lives, but now more than ever parents need a basic guide that tells them everything they need to know and provides the answers they are seeking in a simple, effective fashion. This book will do just that for the parent looking to help their child while at the same time empowering them to make their own sound decisions as they grow and face challenges that lie ahead of them.

Discover how your child's mind develops and influences every action. Learn to identify behavioral issues before they fully develop and repair the ones that have become problematic. And, most of all, learn the key to help your child reach success and happiness in life.

The Change

JIM DUDAS

Jim Dudas was born in Vietnam. Adopted in 1975 through the "Operation Baby Lift," a program sponsored by President Ford that evacuated over 2000 children out of Saigon. He was raised by an American family in northern New Jersey with two brothers and one sister. Jim has earned a B.S. in Accounting from Bryant University in Rhode Island. He has over 20 years of strategic financial planning experience in the fashion industry and has worked with top companies including Tommy Hilfiger, NYDJ and Buffalo Jeans.

Jim has also completed his certification of the "Trainer's Academy" a powerful program facilitated by John Hanley Sr., of the Leadership Training and Development Group. John Hanley Sr. is the original founder of the Lifespring Trainings. Worldwide millions of people have participated in these workshops since the 1970's.

Jim has recently founded Whatever the Fashion LLC, a consulting company providing leadership training, coaching and business services. Jim is considered by many the best "results" leadership trainer coach in the Tri-State Area.

GAME CHANGER

By Jim Dudas

When you think of the Game Changers in today's world, who comes to mind? Do you think of Jeff Bezos of Amazon, changing the way we shop; Mark Zuckerberg, the founder of Facebook, changing social media and the way we communicate; pro athlete Magic Johnson, changing the game of professional basketball; Warren Buffet, one of the most successful stock investors who is in the top 1% of the wealthiest people worldwide; Madonna, the queen of pop music, changing the landscape of a traditional performance artist; or Oprah Winfrey, a media mogul who impacted lives through television? These are people who are at the top of their game and have influence, impacting tens of millions of people worldwide.

Whether we realize it or not, we have all influenced each other in one way or another, sometimes in positive and negative ways, directly and indirectly. Everyone grows up and creates his own sets of beliefs and values and assumptions. Everyone's view of the world is influenced be his parents, his education, the places he has lived, the relationships with other partners and their experiences.

We often live our lives on autopilot, making decisions thinking it will change our future destination. Although we feel like we have choices, these choices are confined by the culture in which we are born. So we operate with our destination already predetermined for us and we feel stuck, like caught in a drift… feeling like no matter what we do, we will end up in the same place.

Looking as far back over the last 42 years of my life, or as far back as I can remember, I operated in this cultural context, or drift, of "that's just the way it is." I felt stuck in my life, like there was no way out and had no control of the way things would turn out. I probably felt this way most of my life.

I was born in Vung Tau, Vietnam, in 1971, during the Vietnam War. At the age of 3, I became an orphan and was placed at Holt International Children's Services. My birth father returned to his own family and my birth mother no longer could care for me, due to her health conditions. During the fall of Saigon in April 1975, I was adopted into an American family through President Gerald Ford's "Operation Babylift." This was a program in which more than 2,000 orphans were evacuated from South Vietnam to the United States and other countries, including Australia, France and Canada.

I was adopted into an American family with two biological children, and three years after my arrival we had a fourth child in our family. We lived in Ho-Ho-Kus, a small but very affluent town in northern New Jersey. It was clear to me from an early age that I was adopted, since I was the only Asian in the family and one of the few Asians in town.

The earliest memories I have are back when I was around 4 or 5 years of age. I have no memory of Vietnam whatsoever. My family upbringing centered around the core values of getting a college education, working hard, saving money and being with family.

Grownups and family friends frequently told me how lucky I was to be adopted, living here in New Jersey with a great family. I always politely agreed with them, but subconsciously I was thinking, "Are you serious? You have no idea what it is like to be me. You have never been in my shoes and you don't know how I feel!" In my world and in my experience growing up, I definitely was not like, nor did I feel like, everyone else. I felt I was inferior to everyone else. I was nothing like my brothers and sister. I was the only adopted child. I was the only one who had to experience what it was like being a different race and being 20% smaller in size compared with my peers.

On top of that, I was hard of hearing. I was a very easy target to be picked on and bullied. Even though it wasn't very cool that my younger sister had to stick up for me, I was very appreciative. I think it is fair to say that I was not the most popular kid in school, nor did I have a lot of friends.

My family also did not have a lot of discretionary income. We were among the poorest of the rich in our neighborhood. I saw the world of the "haves" and the "have nots" in terms of material possessions: name-brand clothing, new dirt bikes with mag wheels, spending money to go downtown for lunch, expensive birthday parties, and new electronic video games. I had to work for everything I wanted and felt jealous of everyone else who seemed to have everything handed to them. Life seemed so much better for them.

I had many times complained and asked why: Why was I adopted? Why did my birth parents give me up for adoption? Why can't I hear like everyone else? Why do I have darker skin and slanted eyes? Why can't I get nice clothes, a new bike or a nice birthday party? Why am I so deprived? The answer I often received was that "life is just not fair." I often felt that this was just the way it was and I had no control over my life. I thought I always would be inferior and never really amount to anything in my life. I don't think my childhood was any better or worse than any others, but those were just challenging experiences that created my beliefs out of which I lived my life.

In my generation, we were taught to believe that you must do several things to become successful and happy: study hard to get straight A's in grade school through high school in order to get into a good college, get a good job, make a lot of money, get married, buy a nice house and have children. Then teach your children to do the same and live happily ever after.

So that's what I did. Well, not exactly. I managed to get inducted in the National Honor Society in high school and get into a decent college.

My parents sent me off with a car and they paid my college tuition plus room and board. I earned an accounting degree and landed a good career in the fashion industry, earning decent money. I purchased a house and got married. Fifteen months later I got divorced. I did not have children. Even though I made these choices, I believed at the time that I was in control of these decisions. In reality, these choices already were in the deck of cards that had been dealt for me. I recently just realized this about 4 or 5 years ago after I had taken a series of personal development/transformation seminars. I became very aware of the things I do, why I have been doing them, who I was in the past, how I have been thinking and how I currently am living my life. I became aware on many different levels that my underlying beliefs or my subconscious mind was on automatic pilot, and I did most things by habit. These habits and underlying beliefs were preventing me from getting what I wanted out of life. I had discovered what had been missing from me and what my purpose was for living.

During these seminars, I had a pivotal moment or a quantum leap in the conversations of my subconscious mind that had instantaneously shifted my way of being, my beliefs, and my interpretations of the way I observed the present moment. I was propelled into a future space that created results that I once had believed to be impossible. I am not talking about incremental steps or improving on what already exists, like taking small steps from point A to point B. I'm talking about game-changing results that would not have happened without this pivotal moment. I learned this instantaneous shift can be practiced and we all have the power to do so.

I was able to completely let go of all my limiting beliefs at different moments and propel myself into a new direction to obtain my goals and desires. In doing so, I have created many new beliefs and experiences.

I created a clear understanding and experience of what appreciation really is. One cannot appreciate without knowledge of that subject matter or person or event. I learned to appreciate all the powers that are given to us: the ability to see, hear, touch, smell and feel. We have to the ability to think, learn and dream.

If you really think about it, these are all miracles in themselves. We often live each day without appreciating these gifts. We spend much of the day being judgmental, angry, resentful, pitiful or feeling victimized. I learned to appreciate my family and friends, my career, my skills, life, even my past and who I am today. Appreciation is a two-way street, requiring the willingness to give and receive appreciation. It requires letting your guard down – disregarding preconceived judgments in order to fully accept the vulnerability to give appreciation away.

I also learned the importance of intimacy, but not the kind of intimacy you have with your lover. The intimacy I am talking about is the personal connection of creating oneness with others. Although we are all individual people with different tastes, we operate such as there is no separation of who we are. Allowing others to be intimate with me requires me to be open and vulnerable. At the same time, I must be compassionate with them and be aware of their sufferings and pain.

I would like to emphasize this also requires generous listening; listening to understand without judgment and without my own agenda. The value of intimacy is the ability to relate on a deep level with others and understand one another. When I create intimacy, I create trust to move forward.

But one of the most important things I realized that was missing was that I was playing a very small game in this so-called game of life. I was responsible for holding myself back in life. I have so much more potential that is not being realized, ability to support and make a huge difference in others, ability to dream big with new possibilities for myself and others and the world. I discovered that it is not okay with me that there are children living with hunger, violence and drugs. I created a vision bigger than just myself where every child "gets" to grow up in a loving family filled with love, joy and passion.

I made the decision to be different and changed my beliefs about who I am and what is my purpose. I decided to live my life with a vision for the world, appreciation of life, and intimacy of truly connecting with others. I became a game changer starting with my own personal world first. I took that leap of faith - trusting myself and creating a mindset that everything is possible - the ability from within me to move, touch and inspire my own world and the world of family, friends and all people of the world.

I asked friends and family to provide me with feedback in order to collect evidence to support my progress and stay aligned with my vision. Listed below are some of the responses received:

"11 years ago you always took care of yourself first and dismissed your family. You often did not engage or communicate at family functions. You were often rude and selfish or didn't want to be a part of our family.

Today, you now make being together seem so special, that it is not an obligation, but a desire to be with us; you now converse with our guests and are very pleasant to be around. You are able to open up and share your feelings and love. We see how you've grown into a fuller person, a caring person, one who is willing to give time to his parents, his brothers and sisters, his nieces and nephews. It is like you finally realized that you are an important part of the family and have claimed your rightful place in the family lineup!"

"I've seen you evolve as a person and as a coach. You look to grow and question what you think you know, and give yourself space to evolve. You are calm and listen, and are a space of reflection. You seem to have become more grounded in yourself and your purpose. You don't pick and choose where you use this work, you bring this work into all aspects of your life and therefore into the lives of the people around you. You are the space of change, evolution and growth, with ease and grace."

"In the past, you were less engaging with people. Today, I see you as someone who is confident with a strong sense of identity and self-awareness… polished; and as someone who is guided by a strong sense of moral integrity."

"You have been such an awesome brother and uncle to my children! You became a part of our family and had such a tremendous impact and everlasting effect on the dynamics of our family and on my life as well!"

"Since I first met you, you have become much more relaxed. You tackle the things you can control with purpose. You don't sweat the small stuff. You're more optimistic. You're more introspective.

You take an active interest in helping others. This brings you joy. I've watched you help some people start to believe that they can "have it all" through self-awareness, determination, hard work and dedicated focus. I believe that the best investment someone can make is in their own personal development. You're a testament to that and I expect that people will experience that through your story."

I don't share this feedback to impress anyone but rather to illustrate that anyone has the potential to become a game changer. You, too, can get feedback and collect evidence, showing that you can make a difference and have a purpose. I believe there are far too many people out there living their lives, just as I did, limiting their potential and living a life based on their circumstances; lacking the recognition that their beliefs are their own constraints. Changing their mindset would allow them to live a more fulfilling life.

You, too, can be a game changer and be at the top of whatever you desire. You can make sudden and significant changes in your own world and in the lives of others. Your age, where you come from, education level, ethnic background, or whatever your current situation may be, is irrelevant.

I invite you to take an opportunity to really look at your own life and think about what are your current limiting beliefs, events, and habits that are holding you back.

Perhaps the baggage from a relationship that went bad, those expectations that are never meet, the dependence on others for happiness, or that anger and resentment from those who did you wrong. Think about what you decided about these beliefs, events and habits that you are holding to be true for you. You know the stories you keep telling yourself to support the way you feel. By letting go, imagine how free and liberated you would feel!

What if you could learn how to redesign your beliefs and habits to empower you to create unprecedented life changing results? Would you learn how? What if you could uncover hidden talents and gifts that could influence and change others. Would you be compelled to do so? What if you could fully experience and be engaged in life with heartfelt commitments with freedom and passion. Would you jump on it? Imagine what the world would be like if we all just decided to do this! I believe we all have this power within us. We can all decide and make this change!

Start now and you could make an impact and change your life and the lives of 5 other people. And if those five people made a difference with five others, and so on... 25, 125, 625, 3125 repeated ten times.

That would be over 2.4 million lives that changed! Take that quantum leap and decide to make a difference through vision, appreciation and intimacy. How would you like to be the catalyst that forever changes the lives of others!

Contact Info

Jim Dudas

JimDudas@gmail.com

www.wtfconsultingnyc.com

203-803-7512

The Change

DR. TIANNA CONTE

Tianna is a unique blend of mystic and scientist; naturopath, interfaith minister, initiated shaman and mind-body therapist. She has been empowering people in personal evolution for forty years. Integrating ancient wisdom with cutting edge energy psychology has earned her a reputation as a "physician" to the soul.

Her Near Death Experience uniquely qualifies her to bring a deep intuitive knowledge of consciousness, life, death, and transformation to the eternal journey.

Tianna focuses on training others to live life with passion, purpose, and pleasure. She is the director of Infinite Possibilities Productions, co-founder of Ageless Secrets, and best-selling author of *Love's Fire*. She is the producer whose story is featured in Awaken Your Riches, and co-stars in Dying To Live. Currently in private practice, she conducts retreats in NY and CA, travels, lectures, and participates with shamans and spiritual masters, pioneering ways for people to explore the evolutionary power of love-based living.

REV M. AZIMA JACKSON, MS, DMin

Azima uses energetic healing, song, meditation, counseling, and ceremony for life's rites of passage. This leads to greater self-discovery and re-invention. She is an ordained Interfaith Minister who holds a Doctorate in Ministry, Masters in Divinity from Yale Divinity School, and Masters in Biological Sciences. Chopra University recognizes her as Vedic Master: certified to teach Primordial Sound Meditation, Yoga, and Perfect Health. She is a Reiki Master and has served as Chaplain at both Yale New Haven and Griffin Hospitals. Azima is well versed in both Eastern and Western approaches to music. She is a certified Leader of the Improvisional Music Organization, Music for People. She has produced two CDs, *Passages Through Light* and *Angel Love*. Azima is Director of House of Light and co-founder of Ageless Secrets. She is co-executive producer of the documentary, Awaken Your Riches. She conducts retreats in CT and CA.

EXTRAORDINARY JOURNEY

Conversations Between Two Worlds

By Dr. Tianna Conte & Rev Azima Jackson

"Those who are awake live in a state of constant amazement." - Buddha

What do the words "extraordinary journey" mean to you? What images or wisdom come to mind? Are you enjoying and relating to your life as extraordinary? For us, the word "extra" stands out and becomes extra-ordinary.

What we know to be true is for an extra-ordinary journey there needs to be something extra. What do you believe goes into the extra? For us, the extra is living beyond the five senses. This is living as if the mind was a sixth sense as noted by quantum physicist Fred Alan Wolf, in the movie we produced, *Awaken Your Riches*. This awareness was exemplified super-naturally by Tianna's NDE (Near Death Experience) and by Azima's mortal encounter with death. The polarity of these experiences became the foundation of the messages and principles that Tianna and Azima are here to share. The essence is in accessing the guidance and invisible power that is available to all of us.

Everything is perception. It is our perception that can keep us small or beckon us to evolve. Everything is energy as proven by quantum physics. Many have heard… "glass half empty, glass half full." Einstein states it best, "There are two ways to live: You can live as if nothing is a miracle; you can live as if everything is a miracle."

Are you aware of the magnificence of who you are? To perceive oneself through mere mortal eyes of body - limited by skin boundaries, and brain - limited by thoughts and beliefs taken from pre-birth to age 8, would be a travesty. Intuitively, as children we all engage in the magic of possibilities. Unfortunately, for many this is conditioned out through well meaning parents and authorities who want to raise us to the ways of the world. They project their limitations on us as if they are the experts. The biggest fallacy is now continued.

We are here to erase the limitations placed on us and take back our divine destiny as stated best in the words of the French philosopher, Pierre Tielhard de Chardin, "We are not human beings having a spiritual experience. We are spiritual beings having a human experience."

We are bigger than we appear to be. We are talking about beings of frequency that are beyond what we can experience by the five senses. Tianna intuitively knew this, and her near death experience (NDE) in 1995 proved it to her. Without getting into the details, her NDE was not through accident or disease. It was through a body wrap meant to de-stress. This story can be found in *Love's Fire: Beyond Mortal Boundaries*. Hearing the following words, and an invitation to a life review, forever changed Tianna's perception. Her life was enhanced indelibly. Our desire is to enhance your life as well, without the need for a NDE.

"Birth and death are the same. One is celebrated and one is feared. One is celebrated because it is known; one is feared because it is unknown… but both are about essence. One is essence taking on form and the other is essence leaving form behind, returning to Oneness. But both are the same.

The period of time between what is birth and what is death is called life. It is about experiences, experiencing many things, unfolding the truth of one's nature, of expanding awareness of who you really are and the gifts you bring... discovering that love is a frequency, not an emotion. Only love is real. All else is appearance, a part of the illusion created by the senses, and the illusion of separation. Each person is in physical form to give and receive love and so therefore expanding the truth of one's being.

Soon after the above words, what proceeded to unfold was a review of my life. It started from pre-birth and spanned the years to my present age. It came in the form of movie vignettes. I experienced each event of agony - not necessarily agonizing pain, but a painful memory. I experienced what I had felt, what I had thought about it, the choices and decisions that I had made... all of it. However, this is where they had an uncanny twist. I witnessed the memories with no judgment, as if I were watching the unfolding of a perfect script.

As if by divine magic, light penetrated these memories, almost dissolving them. This light uncovered a picture far greater than my mind could have fathomed. Somehow the light of that presence shone through to reveal that each occurrence held within it a gift that was greater than the pain of the experience. As such, these memories of agony could be viewed as growing pains. Indeed everything, bar none, served... regardless of my own judgments. Every one of my experiences had a purpose in some divine design. I feel confident in saying that those moments that cause the greatest pain can also contain the seeds of our spiritual awakening."

As a therapist and shaman, Tianna realized that as we go over and over the pain of our life story, we solidify it's limiting beliefs rather than releasing them and triumphantly transforming them. What we need to do is experience the pain fully and release it as soon as we are capable. Her quest became the desire to pass the gift of a life review on to others, without the liability. Not knowing or getting logically caught up in the "how to," she trusted that all would be revealed. Eventually she met a doctor whose audio CDs addressed the issues in an effortless way. This became the first piece of the puzzle.

Together they designed a journey that is a cross between a vision quest and a life review; empowering people to shift to a foundation based on life enhancing beliefs. Since each person is unique in their memories and experiences, the work is customized, and takes them from pre-birth, through the birthing experience, childhood, culminating in Maslow's hierarchy of basic needs fulfilled in the present.

As the universe would have it, the gifts of the NDE continued to manifest and pass on to others in ever expanding ways. Clearly ensconced in the knowing that all is frequency, and we are that, a friend introduced Tianna and Azima to a computerized energy based machine. This energy machine uses modern technology and an ancient prayer modality known as the Tibetan prayer wheel, to access the benefits of a higher frequency and divine possibilities. This tool is used to take one's intentions, to release subtle energy blocks, and to send blessings and prayers for transformation. This technology works with a full-length photo of the person requesting balancing. It bathes your picture with vibrations that first clear and then balance your energy field as it subtly reduces stress. As we were writing this, Tianna realized that the energy machine is the closest to duplicating, on autopilot, an invisible power to dissolve the blocks that blind one's perception of the divine blueprint - similar to her NDE. Go to http://www.age-lesssecrets.com

Tianna's "aha" moments continued as she realized another piece of her NDE puzzle had unfolded. She had recalled that during her NDE she was bathed in a Light and frequency of Love that was beyond words, and "the peace of God which passes all understanding" (John, Bible). Upon hearing this, Azima was inspired to mention the quote from 1 John in the Bible that says, "God is love."

At this point, Tianna played with the words she heard in the NDE. "Love is a frequency, not an emotion." For the first time, she expanded it to say, "God is a frequency, not a religion... God is Love." This awareness rang true for both of them, and they became humbled in it's message. The famous quote of Rumi came alive, "I belong to no religion. My religion is Love. Every heart is my temple."

To our amazement, as we continued to craft this chapter, we witnessed the biggest piece of the NDE puzzle come into visibility. Despite her hesitancy, Tianna felt pressed to express the memories of the trauma and tragedy that happened when she was thirteen years old. The essence, without the details, is that Tianna's father (hero, doctor/mentor) died, and she was sexually violated the same day by a trusted relative. We both recognized that this sacred wound was crying out to deliver the ultimate message that Tianna had heard energetically and never understood - "In time, Truth will be revealed."

Although the young Tianna had raged in agony at the force called God during her darkest hours, she had been embraced by an energy of Love that filled her with an ecstasy of Light. It was similar to that experienced in her NDE decades later. She had also heard, for the first time, the voice of guidance as a loving power that she affectionately related to intimately as God. The first words were:

"Surrender, Each day, Step by step, You will be shown the way"

- Love's Fire: Living the Awakened Journey

Speaking and listening to this voice became a daily discipline and undergirding to transforming Tianna's life from tragedy to triumph! Accessing this awareness became the foundation of a life's calling that spanned forty years of empowering others through her gifts. Her longing had always been to set people free from self-imposed limitations and dependency on outside guidance.

This force had mystically aligned Tianna to perceive and live life from the inside out. She realized that most people were conditioned to live life from the outside in. Her burning desire became, "How could this wisdom and transformational shift be passed on?" The humorous answer to her prayer was through the bite of a poisonous brown recluse spider on our land in Costa Rica.

As Tianna's healing journey progressed with a combination of minimal medical intervention coupled with innate wisdom, a system emerged. Each day, as she peered and applied the cream and gauzed the deep holes in her toes created by the spider's poison eating to the bone, a vision appeared. One step, each day for five days, followed by five more days of hand signals and gestures, and a seeming miracle unfolded. Not only were Tianna's toes made whole, so was the code made manifest for others to take their steps with a simple blueprint for guidance and power. The same words Tianna heard at thirteen could be duplicated for all!

We are honored to introduce this system, affectionately called the GPS Code. The acronym GPS is God Positioning System for those who are comfortable with God as a frequency of Love; for others, Guidance Power System.

We grappled with revealing the 5 gears and hand signals at this time. As Azima and I continued to dialogue, what emerged was an awesome awareness that the seed to the GPS Code was hinted at in what I heard mystically: "Surrender, Each day, Step by step, You will be shown the way." We marveled that the daily discipline and two of the five gears were obvious in this quote. At this point it was evident that it would not be in the highest and best interest to you, the reader, to get a sketchy look that could not be easily applied.

Yes, they are called gears for a greater reason that takes you beyond steps. The gears appear simple, yet are significantly more than they appear to be. If you desire a deeper understanding and fuller experience of this GPS Code, we are thrilled take you to your next level. Please visit http://www.gps-code.com and enjoy the trip called evolution!

We can assure you that by setting your innate GPS, your soul will be in the driver's seat of your own vehicle. As with your car, this system will set your destination to the best solution of your problem, shifting you from self-sabotage to self-empowerment. In the words of Einstein, "When the solution is simple, God is answering."

One of the undisclosed gifts that Tianna received in the NDE is that the chatter of her "monkey mind" was silenced. Passed on through the GPS Code is this ability to quiet your mind, as well as a simple way to release your emotions so they are expressed, rather than repressed or suppressed. In essence, it's about shifting from reactive living to creative for an extraordinary journey.

Feeling fulfilled at a level that defied her conscious mind, Tianna embraced that her NDE had given her the pieces for a sneak peek into the bigger picture of her life. As Azima listened to these profound revelations, she was awestruck and speechless as to, "Now What!" Tianna urged her shocked friend to be patient and compassionate with herself, as Azima, and in turn, connect with her heart and express her truth. The starting point for Azima was her affinity and guidance through music and sound healing.

As we discoursed and mused over the expansiveness of human consciousness, a memory came up for Azima. She remembered her Indian singing teacher once describe Indian music as having no beginning and no end. While twenty-two notes are audible to the physical ear in Indian music, the intervals between these notes are microtonal. Her teacher had referred to entering worlds in these minute intervals, or vast states of consciousness, psychological and emotional, where the music took her. If we look at life as vibration, the reality is that there is no beginning and no end. We both saw this as a metaphor for life.

We acknowledged that sound could be the bridge between form and invisible energy; between the manifest and the abstract. Azima's Indian music teacher further saw music as a path to self-realization. As we explored this possibility, the following quote came to mind, "In the beginning was the Word, and the Word was with God, and the Word was God" (John, Bible). Azima realized that if one sees God as vibration, as the frequency that breathed and continues to breathe us into existence, then it would make sense that sound/music would be a pathway to our authentic Selves.

She took a quantum leap in her own evolution by realizing that God is beyond form, beyond masculine and feminine. An ecstatic Tianna chimed in, "Anyone that gets this understanding, sets themselves free." At this point, Azima referred to a quote from her mentor in spirit and Sufi mystic-musician, Hazrat Inayat Khan, "They have said that the soul entered the body through music. In private, they have said that the music itself was the soul."

Azima began her own conscious review of how important music had been to her since childhood. In so many ways it had been her gateway to her soul's guidance. As Tianna pressed her for more information, what started to unravel was the story of Crohn's Disease and how Azima nearly died several times. Although Azima admitted that medicine helped her, she eventually began to be more frightened of the medicine than the disease itself. So she began looking for alternatives or complimentary modes of healing. This is when her spiritual journey began to expand, and the following poem emerged:

- I woke

- In burst of light

- To see Love's perfection

- A glimmer of eternity

- In you

As the pain of the Crohn's Disease deepened, so did the writings and the music. The turning point piece that Azima was hesitant to share was the Angel song in which she had first felt the palpable love of angels. At that time, she was not ready to share the song because it had an intimacy and love to the likes of which she had never experienced before, and she didn't want to lose that visceral knowing:

> Angels surround me, enfold me with love
>
> Hold me and fill my heart with light and love from above.
>
> Their wings encircle me bringing their peace
>
> Comfort, protect me bringing their peace.
>
> They're with me always, in this I rejoice;
>
> They're with me always, in this I rejoice (*Angel Love* CD)

In retrospect, Azima realized that her physical sickness was a portal opening for her into higher dimensions. It wasn't until many years later that Azima recognized that Crohn's disease had been suppressed emotions that had not been acknowledged, and continued to eat away at her until she began to face them. To listen to her cells, her needs, was part of her journey. This listening took different forms. Music was one.

Because music is vibration, it has the ability to connect directly to the frequency of our emotions. It can release emotions of pain, fear, anger, and bring harmony and peace to one's cells. For Azima, playing an Indian string instrument, the tamboura, and often chanting with it, released pent-up tears. As she continued this form of prayer, she felt nourished by their vibration. So much so, that the accumulation of these chants became a CD, *Passages Through Light,* for others to enjoy; as well as to imprint them in cellular memory.

Is there a musical instrument that you play or music you enjoy, or chants that would evoke thoughts, emotions, or body sensations for you? What would they be? For Tianna, classical music, especially Pachabel, came to mind.

Sounds also affect us in different ways. Toning and humming are simple methods that you can access anytime you need. These can support you with getting in tune with your body and emotions; centering and lowering blood pressure are also benefits. This particular exercise activates the brain, and cleanses every fiber in the body and brain.

Basic humming exercise follows:

- Sit in a relaxed position with your eyes closed

- Purse your lips and make the sound, "shhhhh"

- Hum loudly creating a vibration, particularly toward the front of your face

- Hum a single pitch continuously

- Imagine you are a hollow reed filled with vibrations of humming

- At some point you will become just the listener; the humming will be happening by itself.

- You can do this until you feel a shift

Another powerful form of vibration is chanting. A Tibetan abbot once had talked to Anima about this and described it as prayer, in which the feeling of the chant, with repetition, brings the person to a vibrational level where the request has already been answered.

For Azima, music continues to be her pathway to her soul's voice and to setting her free. In the words of Hazrat Inayat Khan, "Music touches our innermost being and in that way produces new life, a life that gives exaltation to the whole being, rising it to that perfection in which lies the fulfillment of one's life."

These memories had Tianna and Azima sometimes laugh, more often be amazed, at the opposite directions that they have lived into life, into their soul's nature. Tianna, since she was a little girl, had a more energetic, mystical perception of life. Experiencing death through the eyes of a NDE even anchored Tianna more toward the mystical point of view. Azima, on the other hand, in a more physical human way, came close to death at least two to three times and felt only pain, with often little hope. This anchored her into the struggle of the mortal point of view. We agreed that the dance between the mystic and mortal perceptions embraces the totality of life.

We trust that we have imparted wisdom from our extraordinary journey to empower the "extra" in your journey. Our message is that as we each awaken to who we truly are as infinite beings of Light and Love. We are here to live fully and leave a lasting legacy. In opening our mind and joining in the union of our heart, we raise our consciousness. This opens the gateway to the alchemy of personal and planetary transformation that is the ripple affect of awakening and an extraordinary journey for all! The words of Lao Tzu exemplify it best:

> "If you want to awaken all of humanity then awaken all of yourself. If you want to eliminate the suffering in the world then eliminate

all that is dark and negative in yourself. Truly, the greatest gift you have to give is that of your own transformation."

CONTACT INFORMATION:

www.age-lesssecrets.com

info@age-lesssecrets.com

914-200-4369

www.infinitepossibilitiesproductions.com

drtianna@gmail.com

914-205-4969

www.facebook.com/tiannaconte

www.linkedin.com/in/drtianna

www.ahouseoflight.com

info@ahouseoflight.com

203-453-0213

www.facebook.com/maryazima

www.linkedin.com/pub/mary-azima/8/90/b18/

The Change

FLORA SOFIA

Flora Sofia is a model and actress with 8 years of experience in the entertainment industry. An accidental model as she refers to herself, she has done several print and video campaigns, was runner up Miss Brazil USA in San Diego, she is often found on the runway, on set or hosting an event. Flora has been empowering her friends and family for several years and now teaches women's empowerment to women of all walks of life worldwide as the creator and founder of The Beautiful Power™. The Beautiful Power has grown into one of the most sought after women's coaching organizations in the world. Flora has the ability to turn her students into vibrant, confident women in just a few interactions.

THE BEAUTIFUL POWER

By Flora Sofia

I am going to introduce you to something that all women have but many haven't discovered. This is something that once you discover, befriend, and nurture, it will change your life in a way that you'll never want to go back to not having it.

I grew up in a humble background in Brazil. I am one of many members of a highly intellectual family of professors, professionals, and entrepreneurs. If you are from Brazil, or have lived and worked there, you know that nothing comes around easily. As a matter of fact - more often than not - you'll find yourself working really hard and making little progress very slowly, since the country is unfortunately infested with corruption. Although my parents were attorneys, I didn't grow up in luxury. During many years, we lived with a very tight budget. We had enough for the essentials, and at times – although my mom as a single parent didn't want to make any mention of it – had to brace for harder times. I am the youngest of 3 kids, and felt on my skin and in my soul what the hard times can do to someone when they don't have a strong structure.

In my particular environment, we had a much divided family. My mom had the kids and was responsible for all that concerned us. My dad had a life partner, a fourth child, and never paid child support. The life partner was on a mission to win the game; and used very low, evil, and desperate measures to assure that she would. Growing up in that environment was not easy. I had no sense of self-esteem, self-worth, or hope that I could be successful. My life had always been about surviving and when I achieved a particular level of maturity as a teenager, I started working and co-providing for my family. I did what I had to do because the circumstances demanded it. Having embraced the role of "fixer" at very young age and being under constant pressure to meet everybody's expectations sucked the life out of me, and I grew to become a very unhappy young woman.

At 23, I reached the breaking point. I couldn't function sanely any longer and had to do something to leave that hardship behind. In my mind I had four options: 1) go to Spain to get a Master's degree (I had just obtained a BA in Spanish), 2) seek refuge at a cousin's place is southern Brazil, 3) join my boyfriend in his quest for a better life in the U.S., or 4) walk myself into a mental institution. Little did I know that my destiny's destination was the United States!

The first 2 years living abroad - learning and understanding the new culture and figuring out what I wanted to do - were far from easy, but were very rewarding as they paved the way for something very important to happen. On the horizon, there was the possibility of growing out of being the sad, lost, pain-ridden girl I had been for all my life. From the third year on, I embarked on the adventure of what I called "inner house cleaning." From the moment I started this adventure, my life changed tremendously. I participated in a beauty pageant (Miss Brazil USA) and placed as runner up, people left and right asked me if I was a model, friends told me I needed to be on television... The more internal change I did, the more it reflected outwardly, and the greater happiness I found.

I think that this is a process that will only end when I am ready to bail out of planet Earth, therefore I am constantly seeking to find little old stuff to clean up. We humans are an amazing race, and if we are not growing we are dying. And we have too much life, light, and power to walk around dormant and be a product of our past by default.

There is something I call The Beautiful Power. To my joy, I have found that I have it... and that every woman has it. It is not about skin deep beauty, it goes much, much deeper. It's about the gem you are, while you don't even know it. I am excited to share this with you and witness your growing into your Beautiful Power and having an incredible life. This is your time to understand who you are, what you want, and how to grow to be an incredible woman others look up to (your siblings, your parents, your relatives, your friends…). What I found is that many women can realize that they have an incredible and irreplaceable power: to bring light and beauty to the world. My vision is to see as many women as possible create a world where we decide what flies and what doesn't - from the premise of being light bearers. As with most greatness, it all begins with a simple story…

Once upon a time there was a sweet little girl who was scared of the world. She learned really, really young that the world wasn't to be trusted, nor were people, nor was she. She saw and felt so much sorrow and yet didn't want to see any of it. She cried and asked for it to stop but it wouldn't. She couldn't help but think: "If they knew how bad this is for everyone… " She realized she couldn't win. She realized she was too small, too ugly, and too unimportant. She realized she wasn't put in the world to win. Others could. Others would. Not her. She grew so frightened and small that one day she disappeared. The little girl was replaced by sadness, obligation, guilt, and responsibility. Where once used to be a sweet little girl, there was no trace of her left.

Many moons later, the little girl of my heart came back. She had heard me say: "You are OK. You are my baby. You are beautiful my sweet angel, and I love you. Nothing and no one will ever hurt you again. You are mine." And she hasn't left my sight since.

You have the power and the responsibility to be whoever you want to be. These are unique times as they differ from how things used to be 40, 50, 60 years ago and from how things will be in 5, 10, 20, 30 years from now. How your life will be then… it's up to you to start creating it, right now. In today's day and age, women face a tremendous amount of pressure to be pretty, to prove themselves to their family members and to the world, to fit in, to show men that they can open the car door themselves. The very sad part of it is, that as if following the herd, we women don't question why we live life the way we do. Like being hypnotized, we don't question or analyze things, people, and situations from our own minds. We pass judgment. We act appropriately to avoid being judged and chastised. We do as it's expected from us. Someone created the rules and the codes of conduct; someone wrote a book with rules that we must follow, otherwise things will get ugly. But who are they? What do they know about you?

Don't get me wrong. It's not OK to approve or condone wrongful actions, crime, abuse, or things of the like. One can easily discriminate the good (that which promotes grace, love, and joy) from the bad (that which creates pain, suffering, and anger), right? Common sense has us understand that: 1) if it will enhance yours or someone else's life, then do it. 2) If it will cause you or someone else pain and suffering, then don't do it.

I'll tell you one sure thing: if you live your life meeting someone else's expectations, abiding by what the authority figures in your life have determined for you, bending over backwards and turning into a pretzel to fit the model of perfect beauty, you will not be happy. Why? Because none of it is about you. None of it is about who you are or about what your innermost desire is. They have set the rules because it was convenient to them or because it created a result they wanted. Look, I didn't want to be a miserable child. I didn't want to be unsure about my worth. And I didn't want to be lonely. But I had someone in my life tell me that because I am a child of a divorced mixed woman, I am not good; because I have a fro, I am not pretty; because I am not white, I will not succeed. Was that true? It was. For as long as I believed in it, it was true. Miss Brazil USA came and went and I didn't see my beauty. I believed so much in the rotten lies that "someone" had told me decades ago, that I questioned the judging panel's sanity! So rest assured, that there is someone in your life that has planted a funny seed in you that has got you too shy to shine.

Question, girl. Question everything. Questioning will set you free because it will allow you to find out for yourself what's right for you. Once you find out for yourself, you have your power in your hands; you are no longer doing things because they want you to, because you have an image to fit, or because you are avoiding punishment. Can you think about worse punishment than being miserable with yourself?

You will find happiness once you live in harmony with who you are and don't let anything get in the way of it. You are worth it. You are worth being happy. You are worth being your best friend. You are worth living your life however the heck you want, as it will make you feel good about yourself! You might as well just to it! Just imagine yourself at a great party, with great music playing on the background, surrounded by great friends, and you dancing the soles of your shoes away! No one else is dancing and it's not your problem. Your business is to do what makes you happy. So go on! Dance away! Shake your bones and turn up the most beautiful curve (your smile). You will walk away from that party so ecstatic you'll ask yourself how come you don't do this more often. FYI, people will not call you ridiculous. They will admire you because you dared to make yourself happy in front of everyone! Sexy, huh?

Speaking of sexy. Let's talk about your body. You know? Your perfect body? If you felt uneasy just now, I want you to take a deep breath and open up to the idea that your body – just as it is right now – is perfect. Wait, but only super models' bodies are perfect, right? Nope! Yours is. You have, right now, a perfect body that does exactly what it has been designed to do. You can move around, communicate, breathe, think, cry, you have a heart beating in your chest, and you can smile, so you have it all. Use what you've got. The super model has a perfect body that fits a particular standard today. Marilyn Monroe had a perfect body that fit a particular standard in the 60s. The Greek muses had a perfect body that fit the standard of beauty in the 2nd century, AD. The standard of perfection only fits one category: the standard. Therefore it is limiting. How about you be you and don't worry about fitting in, don't worry about limiting yourself, and just remove the heavy pressure that someone has put on you. How about you go shopping for what makes you feel good before what makes you look good? You have the body you have right now, and it's up to you to beautify it, play with it, change it, use it however you want. As long as you get to glow at the end of the day, it's ok to have the body you have, and it's ok to be you.

In America today, a large share of the population is over-fed and under-nourished. The quality of the processed food available today is poor and it is impoverishing our health. Similarly, the quality of the relationship we have with ourselves is out of balance. On one hand, we consume food to feed our stomach and cover the emotional holes we might have; but don't always look for the best quality foods or evaluate the impact that food has in our health. On the other hand, we engage in relationships to not feel lonely, to have someone there; but we don't evaluate what that person could mean for our future. And it goes beyond… We are who we are, keep being who we be, dream and long to be different, do nothing to change our default patterns, and don't evaluate what we could mean for our future if we keep doing the same old things and being the same old person day in and day out.

Here is a question for you: do you want fit in the current standard of perfection? Why? Are you happy – deep inside – with who you are? Or would you rather find out, from your own delightful relationship with you, what fits well with who you are? I know I sound like that friend that you hate because she is always telling the truth; and you love because she is always telling the truth. But girl, one of the truths I know about life is that the only person that can make you happy is you… not the German chocolate cake, not the boyfriend, not the girlfriend, not your mom, not your dad. We need relationships. We need love. We need to feel good. But most and foremost, we need to be good for, to, and with ourselves. We wake up to ourselves every morning and go to bed with ourselves every night. We are there all the time. We need to learn how to be the person we dream of finding. Only we can give ourselves what we need because only we have known ourselves for as long as we have.

When I talk to people about women's empowerment, their first impression is that I am out to teach women how to be tough, prove themselves to men, how to outsmart the guys, and yell at them for opening the car door. That's not what I am interested in. We have had this standard going on for 5 decades now and we know all about it. I am interested in seeing you shine as bright as you can. Here is a little exercise: the next time you go to a party, notice which girl is the life of the party. She is sassy, vibrant, is the one who is smiling and laughing most, she is fully expressive, she is surrounded by people, and the one having most fun. She is in love with herself. I want that to be you. And I am here to show you how to be her. That is the woman who livens up a room, and with her life she lightens everywhere she goes. She exudes beauty and joy. Her glow is irreplaceable. Men can't do that. Men want that, they crave it, they admire it, they can't take their eyes off it!

Without women, there would be a fully masculine world – one that would be hard, dry, and serious. When women are around there is beauty, softness, and giggles. All the attributes we have: the hair, the eyes, the feminine parts, the soft skin, the feminine voice, are the nectar of life to men. Like flowers bring beauty, color, and fragrance to a garden, we bring beauty, radiance, and life to the world. We have it because it is our power to be the most and foremost expression of beauty. When a woman steps into her own beautiful power she can put a smile on the grumpiest of the faces just because she is there; just because she exists and she is who she is. Other women - who have awakened their beautiful power - can't help but smile when they see the empowered woman walk in the room. She is appreciated and adored. What would it take for you to choose to be this woman? What would it take for you to stop fighting so hard and struggle so much and become the beautiful power? What would it take for you to listen to yourself and lead your life the way you want to, rather than how they want you to? You already have it in you. Let it shine!

Use It

The world will treat you as you let it

They'll tell you who to be

They'll tell you what to do

They'll tell you how to act

They'll tell you what to wear

They'll tell you how to fit in

And if you don't, boo-hoo!

Don't let them shape you

Don't let them shame you

Don't let them define you

Don't let them confine who you are

Don't let them assume who you are not

Don't let your life be run by them

Use your power

Break through

Break free

What they've told you...

Is an imaginary wall

Nothing but a story

Nothing but a myth

You'll believe it if you want to

Or you'll break free from it

Would you?

Could you?

Can you?

How?

Use your power

Use your voice

How could they know so much about you?

They have never been you!

The Change

Don't let them run you

You run you

To the way they treat you or mistreat you

You can say yes, you can say no

Don't take what you don't want

Don't take what harms you

Don't take what doesn't make you happy you

Don't take it because they want you to

Break past the wall

There is a brighter world out there... and it is for you

Use your power

To contact Flora:

www.thebeautifulpower.com

info@thebeautifulpower.com

MARIAH SIEVERS

Internationally celebrated Transformational Coach and Healer Mariah Sievers helps high achieving socially conscious entrepreneurs and world thought leaders accelerate in business and in life.

Her decade long career in the wellness industry has lead Mariah around the world teaching and training other healers, coaches and business owners in holistic wellness practices. Her diverse background in counseling, medical massage therapy, meditation and energy healing has given her a multidimensional approach to assisting others in optimizing their life. She has given over 10,000 healing sessions in award winning resort spas and retreat centers around the world. People are her passion.

THE EDGE OF CHANGE

The Three Elements of Conscious Partnership

By Mariah Sievers

I was on the edge, literally on the edge. The narrow hiking trail barely held space for my two feet as I rocked back and forth on my heels trying to settle the confusion. My nerves were frayed like the wind whipped leaves clinging to the steep ledge. Alone with the evening breeze and mesmerized by the sparkling ocean shimmering up at me, I realized I had done it again. Successfully *failed*. Yes, I had epically and catastrophically failed another long term relationship with a man.

I had been in and out of love before, but this time was different. Every fiber of my being ached. I was raw and undone. My shoe scrapped the edge of the cliff kicking loose gravel down the 60 foot drop.

"How did this happen?" I thought, "I poured myself into this relationship. I gave it everything I had. Time, energy, money, my creativity and all my love. Now what? I feel emotionally bankrupt. I'm physically drained from crying. I'm mentally exhausted, stuck in a spin cycle of what went wrong. Why didn't this work?"

I stared down at the waves slamming the shore and waited on answers that were slow to come. I was shocked that it felt like my life was over, but it was. Our life together was over. I longed for the comfort of the past while balancing on the edge of my uncertain future.

When we started out together, neither of us were looking for a long term relationship. We were driven by our strong chemistry and not really thinking about the future. As the years went on, we formed habits and patterns as a couple. Some were comfort driven and others were magnifications of our unresolved issues. I held a strong belief that no matter what came up, as long as we were willing to work through it then we could continue to grow together. I was about to discover what happens when one partner is all in and the other is one foot out the door.

Just a month before, I was curdled up in the arms of my love, my man, the guy I could see myself growing old with, when he opened his computer and clicked on a message from another woman. She had masterfully captured a completely nude spread eagle selfie. I was too appalled by the photo to appreciate her creative attempts at pornographic seduction. I could feel the shock begin to numb me as I took the computer from his hands scanning it in confusion.

"What... what is this?" I stammered. As I scrolled down, I saw dozens of messages from different women who had sexted and exchanged explicit photos and videos by email.

He wouldn't look at me. It was as if the guilt and shame had chained his eyes to the floor.

"Please tell me what is going on. I need to know," I said quietly.

He remained silent but his body language spoke volumes. We had spent years interpreting each other's moods and facial expressions. Now, there was nothing. He had morphed into a statue of a man behind a brick wall of stalled emotions.

"Why do you have pictures of naked women on your laptop? Who are they? What is this secret email? Wait, you sent pictures of your *penis*? I'm so confused. I don't even know who you are right now."

In less than a minute the illusion of our committed monogamous relationship crumbled under the weight of several years of lying and cheating. I was devastated, disappointed, and disillusioned.

My career as a transformational coach helping others heal from past traumas, release limiting beliefs, and clear emotional blocks, now seemed paradoxical. I was in a relationship with someone who could use my professional guidance, yet I wasn't in a position help him.

The painful memory of that moment overwhelmed me as I slowly backed away from the cliff ledge. Tears splashed down like a gentle summer rain as I continued hiking the trail alone. It was then that I realized how hard it is to end up where you want if you don't know what direction you desire to go. I had not created my last relationship with clarity, so it ended in confusion.

The path of self discovery was paved with uncertainty as I sought the answers on how to create a successful partnership. I interviewed both men and women on the journey to see if they knew why so many of us fail in our relationships and what needed to change. After a year of tears, travel, and honest soul searching, I uncovered three essential elements for cultivating a dynamic partnership: connection, communication, and conscious co-creation.

Connection:

The foundation for a solid long lasting partnership starts with connection. Partnership can be defined as an arrangement in which two parties agree to cooperate to advance their mutual interests. How do you move forward to advance your mutual interests if you don't know what your interests are? Before committing to a long term relationship with another, you have to be willing to commit to the longest relationship of all, the one with yourself.

Cultivating a deep connection to yourself means taking responsibility for your health, attending to your physical and spiritual needs, resolving any unhealed aspects of your past, and providing for yourself materially. It also means identifying your core values, the values that are unshakable and won't change no matter the circumstance.

Dynamic partnership also thrives when each person lovingly attends to their own emotional needs. It's not your partner's job to take responsibility for your emotional state, it's an inside job. What do *you* need to give to yourself so that you feel full of self love? Is it time alone each day to meditate, do yoga, or workout? Is it food that supports your optimal health, or a different sleep schedule? Is it a change in career that allows you to feel on track with your natural gifts and abilities? Taking time to know yourself is vital to maintaining a healthy inner connection so that you can have a healthy outer connection with your partner. When you are taking responsibility for your emotions, you will no longer feel compelled to make demands or place unrealistic expectations on your partner in an attempt to get your needs met from outside of yourself.

There is an outdated model for relationships that says that your partner exists as your "other half," sometimes jokingly referred to as your "better half." Unfortunately, this model carries a subconscious program that you are not complete without your "other." Two people who both believe that they are not complete without each other often find themselves in a co-dependent relationship.

Over the years, I have had several clients come to me suffering from anxiety and depression because they were concerned about finding their "other half." Once they started to see themselves as being whole and complete from within, their stress dramatically decreased. They stopped desperately seeking validation from outside. They started to enjoy their own company. As they formed a deep connection with themselves, dating got easier. They stopped looking at the person sitting across from them as someone who was there to fill an empty space in their life. This shift in perspective helped them move from neediness to clear conscious choice when looking for a partner.

Once you commit to "doing you," or taking care of your needs, then you can turn your attention to "doing" your partner. My ex and I had fallen fast and hard for each other in a flurry of desire. We didn't take time to get to know each other. We were so focused on doing each other that we didn't lay the foundation for a healthy partnership.

It is easy to get lost in a pheromone swirl when you first meet someone you are attracted to. The chemistry can pull you right into their arms. Although great chemistry can lead to great sex, it doesn't always last. Many relationships start because of this magnetic biological pull, and end when the haze of oxytocin lifts. It is then that a couple may realize that they have very few shared interests. Their vision of the future is radically different and they don't know what they ever saw in the person laying next to them.

Sex, past the physical act of carnal pleasure, is a gateway to something much greater; a deep and profound connection with your partner. When two people are well aligned in life and both aware that they have come together by choice, they bring a new level of freedom to their partnership. And freedom is sexy. There is more permission to be open and candid with your partner when you feel free. Sex can reach new levels of pleasure and exploration because each person is actively practicing clear communication and knows what they like.

My ex and I rarely made time to ask each other what the other valued or liked. Instead we fumbled around discovering each other's values whenever we clashed. Conflict became our way to calibrate an opinion of who the other person was. It was painful to realize that we didn't know each other that well even after several years had passed. We connected through lack believing that the "other half" was there to fill our emotional cup, which created a pattern of giving while expecting to get. Even though we loved each other very much, my ex was under the influence of a long standing belief that he wasn't a good person and didn't deserve love. Ironically, on our first date, he said that he was a "bad guy." I choose to see him as a good guy with some "bad" beliefs, but failed to pay attention to the important message he was reinforcing within himself. In the end, he found a way to act out his belief to prove to himself that he was a "bad guy" who didn't deserve my love.

Before entering a new partnership, it is essential to take time to get clear about who you are. Identify and list out your unshakable values. Understand your specific needs, wants and desires. Root out any negative patterns or beliefs that keep you from giving yourself love or receiving it from another. Resolve any issues of lack that may be holding you back. When you stand firmly in who you are, then your partner can do the same. This is the platform for consciously creating what you want. This is the solid foundation where two people come together to share from their overflowing love and accept each other as dynamic and constantly changing.

Communication:

Communication is the framework for creating a healthy holistic partnership. With clear communication we can learn our partner's preferences, their core values, their humor, style, and vision for the future. We can feel loved, supported and heard.

Even after all the centuries of men and women attempting communication, there is still a great deal of confusion when opposite genders try to relate. My relationship was riddled with moments of frustration as we both expected the other to communicate the way we each preferred. He wanted me to "get to the point" and I wanted him to open up and "tell me everything" about his day, or at least more than, "Yah, it was good."

When speaking with the opposite gender, it is easy to fall into the trap of what I call "gender-centric" behavior. When you are being gender-centric, you evaluate the opposite gender according to the standards of your own gender. This is easy to observe in the different styles of opposite gender communication.

For example, as a woman, do you speak "female" when talking to a man? Does the story of your day include *a lot* of details that leave him wondering which part he was supposed to pay attention to? Did you know that men are wired to instinctively use information to solve problems? Somewhere in between "I saw Sarah and then forgot the peaches," when telling him about your recent trip to the store, he got lost wondering why you were sharing this information and what the problem was that you needed help solving.

Masculine energy is logical. It craves order and structure. It wants to maximize time and thrives in efficiency. Keeping communication direct and to the point is efficient communication for the "male" brain.

Men can also exhibit gender-centric behavior. As a man, does your need for efficiency in communication sometimes takes the form of a one word sentence? Have there have been times when your answer wasn't even a word, just a grunt? You may have thought the point was clear, so why elaborate? Just as you prefer a woman to expedite the conversation by minimizing extraneous detail, she would like to hear more than "uh huh" as a reply.

The "female" brain is programmed to share high volumes of information with a meaningful purpose. Women, as the early gatherers, had to relay important info to each other, such as, the berries down by the river with the jagged leaves are poisonous, but the ones growing on the hill with the smooth leaves are safe to eat. For most women, the details *do* matter. It is what kept the village alive. Men, as hunters, could use less words and rely on non-verbal communication while tracking their prey.

Women can effortlessly take in information from multiple sources simultaneously. This bandwidth allows her to process where the children are and what they are doing, what is happening on the TV, count the minutes until the dinner is cooked, write a quick note to schedule an appointment for next Tuesday, and talk on the phone with her friend about the kid's soccer practice. Her thought process allows for integration in multiple directions across non-linear timelines with ease. She can return to an incomplete train of thought an hour later in the same conversation to make sure all of the information regarding that thought is shared.

To better understand ourselves, as well as our partner, we must hold ourselves accountable to how we individually choose to communicate. Breaking the bad habit of gender-centric communication takes practice. When you have cultivated an appreciation for why your partner communicates as they do, it becomes easier to bridge the gap in styles by adjusting the way you communicate. What can you do to modify your default communication style to effectively create clear communication with the opposite gender?

Conscious Co-creation:

With connection as the foundation and communication as the framework, it is naturally fitting that conscious co-creation is the interior design aspect of partnership. It is a fun and joyful space that you both contribute to with your clear vision for the future and shared mutual interests.

What if the new model for creating a dynamic healthy partnership started with each person clearly knowing who they are and what they value, and then openly sharing that with their potential partner? What if we were ready to look at ourselves honestly, and hold ourselves accountable to how we choose to communicate, connect and create?

Conscious dynamic partnership is an ever changing interplay of awareness. It is the space of overflowing love and creativity where two people who are committed to being together - not as halves, but as two solid pillars of strength - can collaborate around a life full of wealth, love, passion and purpose.

When you have taken the time to learn your preferences, celebrate your skills, and clearly define your values, then it is easy to share who you are. When your partner has done the same, then you are both well suited to begin the process of consciously mapping out what it is you would like to co-create. Is it a home? Is it co-parenting? Do you want to create a vacation? Or maybe you both feel inspired to build a business together? Perhaps you simply want to cultivate an incredible synergy that allows you both to feel loved and understood. Because it is a conscious process with clear communication, creativity and deep connection built on mutual interests, and cooperation set with the intention to be dynamic and ever changing, you really have no limits to what your partnership can bring.

My last long term relationship "failure" has become my greatest success. It challenged me to go past my pain and expand my awareness around how I was unconsciously creating my relationship, gender-centrically communicating, and lacking the much needed personal connection for growth.

The beauty in this life is we don't have to keep repeating the patterns of the past once we understand them. As I often say, "Once you know, you can't not know." Look around at your life. Are you on the edge? What needs to change in your relationship to shift it to a dynamic partnership? If you are single, what do you need to do to "do you?" What changes can you activate inside yourself to feel whole and complete, with or without a partner? Any steps you take now will prepare you for your ideal partner, who is somewhere taking their steps to prepare for you.

To schedule your next life upgrade visit her website: www.MariahSievers.com

AFTERWORD

Life is always a series of transitions... people, places and things that shape who we are as individuals. Often you never know that the next catalyst for change is around the corner.

Jim Britt and Jim Lutes have spent decades influencing individuals to blossom into the best version of themselves.

Allow all you have read in this book to create introspection and redirection if required. It's your journey to craft.

The individual and combined works of Jim Britt and Jim Lutes have filled seminar rooms to maximum capacity and created a worldwide demand.

The blessings go both ways, as Jim and Jim are always willing students of life. Out of demand for life changing programs and events, Jim and Jim conduct seminars worldwide as well as created a global company in over 170 countries called Quanta International, that allows anyone to benefit behaviorally as well as financially.

If you would like to hear more about the Quanta company, or to **book Jim or Jim as a keynote speaker for your next special event,** please email our offices at:

quanta@jimbritt.com

Master your moments as they become hours that become days.

Your legacy awaits.

Blessings,

Jim Britt and Jim Lutes

www.ingramcontent.com/pod-product-compliance
Lightning Source LLC
Chambersburg PA
CBHW050632300426
44112CB00012B/1762